LEARNING TO DRIVE

Anthony J. Smith first learnt to drive at the age of twelve when helping a local sports club groundsman who had an old converted ambulance which they used to drive around the field.

In 1964 he began work as a driving instructor with a local driving school and a year later started his own business. He registered with the RAC and the Department of Transport and passed the Institute of Advanced Motorists. He continued as the proprietor of the driving school, employing several instructors, until 1979. Since then he has worked as a Driving Test Examiner for the Department of Transport.

TEACH YOURSELF BOOKS

LEARNING TO DRIVE
for teachers and learners

Anthony J. Smith

Illustrations by Chris Patton

TEACH YOURSELF BOOKS

Hodder and Stoughton

First printed 1980
Second edition 1988

To Shelley, Laura and Paul

British Library Cataloguing in Publication Data

Smith, Anthony J.
Learning to drive: for teachers and learners.—
2nd ed. (Teach yourself books).
1. Automobile driving
I. Title
629.28'32   TL152.5

ISBN 0 340 42517 2

Printed and bound in Great Britain
for Hodder and Stoughton Educational
a division of Hodder and Stoughton Ltd,
Mill Road, Dunton Green, Sevenoaks, Kent,
by Richard Clay Ltd,
Bungay, Suffolk
Photoset by Rowland Phototypesetting Ltd,
Bury St Edmunds, Suffolk

This volume is available in the USA from
Random House, Inc.,
201 East 50th Street, New York, NY 10022

Contents

Foreword

Driving requires a mixture of knowledge, good judgement with manipulative skills, and experienced drivers who daily employ these accomplishments may forget how much there seemed to be to learn when they first started.

Being able to drive, moreover, is so much a need of twentieth century life that it is not surprising that an ever-increasing proportion of the population, not only young people, aspire to acquire the art, and that various facets of the official driving test, the obstacle between learners and qualification, become a frequent topic of modern conversation.

Good instruction and plenty of it is the official recommendation, while the best recipe for success, according to research, is professional instruction with plenty of practice in between. This implies that whether or not learners have professional instruction – and most do have at least some – part at least of their learning and experience-gaining period is going to be under the supervision of an amateur teacher, who although qualified to drive may not have studied teaching the subject in all its details, may subconsciously have acquired undesirable driving habits and who may at the most have a sketchy idea of what the Department of Transport examiner will be looking for during the pupil's official driving test.

Driving is not just a social qualification that one learns for one's own benefit. Being able and qualified to drive is liberating and is extremely useful, but it carries a responsibility to others, to those who will be the present learner's future passengers and even more to the unknown hundreds of thousands of persons who, whether on foot, on horseback, on two wheels or four are the new driver's future co-users of the road.

A serious aspect at the time of writing is that with well over half the candidates for the driving test failing, and some undoubtedly doing so from examination nerves, vast numbers do come to take the driving test long before they are sufficiently prepared or eligible in the examiner's view to be allowed to drive safely on their own. For many years the test failure rate has been well over fifty per cent – in recent years it has averaged fifty-two per cent – and this includes applicants making their second, third or even later attempt. Routine statistics are not kept for first-time passes, but at the most recently announced spot check, in late 1980, fifty-five per cent of test candidates were found to be failing the driving test first time. Allowing for a proportion failing only from nerves therefore, some million people who came for a driving test that year seem to have been insufficiently prepared, wasted at least one test fee and by their sheer numbers helped to extend the long waiting period before they could get a re-test or before others following could have their first test.

The driving test should present few problems to persons temperamentally suitable, with plenty of experience and thoroughly trained to drive. It is quite untrue that most new drivers should expect to fail first time, but it is true that the pupil new to the subject is very dependent upon the teacher, in the content of what is taught, in judgement of the standard reached and in being helped to acquire a sense of confidence, based upon knowledge, experience and safe application, that will not desert the aspiring driver at the moment of taking the test. As well as knowledge therefore, the teacher should have the skill to prepare the pupil to meet all that lies ahead.

Learning to Drive – for teachers and learners is an easily read, sound and well-thought-out book. In conjunction with the official publications on the subject it should prove of considerable help to those who in one way or another wish to be involved in teaching driving, as well as to their pupils who would like to learn.

John Cowan
The Royal Automobile Club

Preface

The old saying 'practice makes perfect' still holds true, especially with learning to drive.

The problem that most people encounter is how to obtain the amount of practice needed to pass the driving test and to go on to become a good, safe driver. To gain enough practice with a qualified professional driving instructor can be extremely expensive. Although some people can learn to drive well enough to pass a test in about 20 one-hour lessons, most need far more than that. Many people need well over 100 hours, which would cost well in excess of £1,000.

With practice from a relative or friend, provided that the correct procedures are followed, improved progress can be made and the whole process of learning to drive becomes more convenient, enjoyable and much less expensive. However, it is vital that both the learner and the amateur instructor are aware of the correct procedures and of the problems that can arise when taking or giving driving lessons. One of the most important aspects of learning is confidence. With extra practice you will gain confidence in your own driving but it is essential that you have confidence in the methods of your instructor.

All professional driving instructors learn their teaching skills over a period of many years. Much of it is trial and error. Through this book the experience that I have gained from teaching numerous people, of all ages, to drive the correct way is passed on to you.

In this book you will find all the information that you require to pass the driving test and to become a very good driver. To enable your friend or relative to help you the book also gives advice on how to teach you to drive correctly and safely. It also contains advice on how to avoid the difficult situations that can arise when instructing on the road.

Introduction

How to get the best use from this book

The first half of the book is set out lesson by lesson so that both you and your instructor have an organised schedule. It is important to do no more in each lesson than is stated, even if your progress appears to be good. It is vital that you acquire a good basic foundation to your driving, especially in such items as clutch control, steering and general 'feel' of the car before trying to advance too much. Extra time spent on these early lessons is well rewarded later, and therefore, if any basic point is not fully understood it should be re-read and practised as many times as is necessary.

The second half of the book is set out on broader lines and can therefore be used more flexibly.

Taking advice from other drivers and learners

You will probably be given friendly advice from other drivers and learners on many aspects of driving and the driving test. Although this advice is usually intended to be helpful it can cause confusion if it contradicts something written in this book. Most of the bad advice concerns the driving test because over the years a sort of 'mystique' has surrounded the test and examiners. Many people relate strange stories about how and why they passed or failed their driving test. These stories are usually exaggerated with the passing of time and are frequently wrong because, under the strain of taking the test, fiction sometimes becomes confused with fact. People often think that they have failed on one particular minor mistake, whereas they have actually failed on something far more serious. Experienced drivers may also tell you certain ways of driving which contradict the way in which you are teaching or being taught.

The first thing to do if this happens is to check again in this book to make sure that it is correct. Although there are more ways than one to do a certain procedure or manoeuvre in driving there is usually only one *correct* way. The correct method is laid down by the Department of Transport and that is the way that the driving examiner expects a candidate to drive on the test. This book is based upon this correct method of driving and later in the book you will find plenty of information regarding the driving test which you will find helpful. Useful information will also be found in the free booklet which is sent to all learner drivers with their first Provisional Licence. This booklet, written by the Department of Transport, is entitled *Your Driving Test and How to Pass it*.

Remember then, it is best to listen and possibly learn from the advice given by other motorists, but beware of its possible inaccuracy.

Using this book without professional instruction

This book is designed to be used without the necessity of any professional instruction or any other instruction books. Together with *The Highway Code* and the booklet *Your Driving Test and How to Pass It*, which are both sent free of charge with the Provisional Licence, this book contains all that is required for a reasonably experienced driver to teach somebody to pass a driving test.

Using this book in conjunction with professional instruction

If you have already had some professional driving lessons and you are now going to have some extra practice with a friend or relation this book will prove invaluable.

How the book is used in these circumstances will depend upon the standard reached when you begin the extra practice. If there has been a good grounding in the professional lessons this book could be started at Lesson 6. On the other hand it would be advisable to begin earlier in the book if there is any doubt about your grasp of the basic control of the car and road procedure. The professional instructor and the amateur instructor who is going to accompany the pupil on the extra lessons will be able to advise on the best starting point.

Using this book if you have previously driven

It depends upon the amount of driving experience you have acquired and the length of time since you have driven to determine the point at which to begin this book. If, as is often the case, there has been only a small amount of driving experience it is advisable to read through Lesson 1 and actually start at Lesson 2. If necessary, however, the course could be started in Lesson 1 at 'precautions before starting the engine'.

Learning to drive on a vehicle fitted with automatic transmission

This book can be used to teach you to drive a vehicle fitted with automatic transmission. The section regarding automatic transmission should be read before the lessons are commenced and the text of the book adjusted accordingly.

Important Points Before Beginning the Course

Instruction mirror

It is important for your instructor to have a separate rear-view mirror, because it will frequently be necessary for him or her to know what is happening behind. Looking round can be awkward and takes too long. An inexpensive mirror with a rubber suction pad can be purchased at most car accessory shops. It should be fixed in a position adjacent to the driver's rear-view mirror.

Seat belts

Seat belts must be worn throughout the lessons by both you and your instructor except when carrying out a manoeuvre which includes reversing (e.g. the turn in the road and reverse exercises). The examiner will normally expect to wear the belt when conducting the test, therefore you should make sure that it is in good working order and that it is easily adjustable. If the seat belt is faulty the examiner could refuse to conduct the test with the consequent loss of the test fee.

Eyesight test

You should make sure that you can read a number plate easily at 23 metres (25 yards) before you begin having driving lessons. If there is any problem you should visit an optician for advice.

Emergency stop

You will find that the emergency stop exercise is not practised until quite late in the book. There are several reasons for this as given below.

1. There may be a tendency for you to misjudge a situation in the earlier lessons. You may think that an emergency stop is needed, whereas some other course of action, by your instructor or yourself, would be safer.
2. It is only after some experience in driving that you will know how and when to use the emergency stop.
3. Once you have almost reached the standard of the test you should find it very easy to do the emergency stop exercise. In fact it is usually only a matter of practising it a couple of times as is explained on page 162 of the course.

The reason that I have mentioned it here is that learners often worry about practising it. They build it up in their own minds from what they hear from other people, into something bigger and more frightening than it actually is. It must be remembered that it is just the same as any normal stop except that it has to be done more suddenly than if you were merely stopping at the side of the road. In other words; instead of being told to stop somewhere in your own time, you have to stop immediately after a prearranged signal (usually the banging down of the instructor's hand on the dashboard, or the examiner in the driving test hitting the windscreen lightly with a book).

How to Read the Course

Preparation notes

Before each lesson there are notes explaining certain aspects of driving to prepare both you and your instructor for the lesson to follow. These notes sometimes also clarify points that may have needed more explaining from the previous lesson. The appropriate notes, therefore, should be studied before each lesson by you and your instructor.

Your instructor can help you both on and off the road and the whole book can be read by both pupil and instructor. The preparatory notes can also be used for revision and should be referred back to as needed. The more frequently they are studied between the lessons, the more progress will be made.

Lessons

At the beginning of each lesson there is information about the type of route to be taken, the maximum duration and what is to be practised during that lesson. At the beginning of some lessons (Lesson 3 for example) there is information concerning possible dangers which your instructor should look out for which should help him to anticipate the problems which might arise.

As stated earlier in this introduction the first five lessons are designed to give you a thorough basic knowledge of driving which is vital to your later progress. It might be necessary to stay on one lesson for two or even three consecutive outings if the progress is not satisfactory. This is not unusual and the effort will be worthwhile in the end.

In the lessons:

*The instructor's dialogue
is written in italics*

Advice to the instructor is
written in a different type face

Advice to the instructor contains very important information about the problems of the instructor and information on any points that may need clarifying.

Before practising on the road the whole lesson should be read several times by your instructor.

You should read the lesson when you get back home. Your instructor should take the written lesson with him in the car, but of course he should not read it while the car is moving. Stop if you or your instructor wish to read anything in the course. (This may necessitate the learning, by the instructor, of short sequences out of the course, such as the changing gear sequence, but this will not prove difficult.)

Advice to the instructor

'Notes for the Instructor' should be studied before the first lesson and revised by the instructor between lessons.

Notes for the Instructor

Understanding the problems of the pupil

One of the essential qualities required to become a good instructor is having an understanding of the problems of the learner driver. The ability and time taken to learn varies greatly between different people. The amount of practice needed depends entirely upon the learning ability of the individual. Remember though, that just because one person learns in 20 lessons and another takes 100, it does not mean that either one is the better driver in the end. The person who takes longer to learn, or finds it more difficult to learn at first, sometimes puts more effort and thought into his driving than the person who found it all too easy.

It is impossible to generalise about the number of lessons needed but you can get a rough guide by considering the learner's age and perhaps his or her previous learning experience. A young person, for instance, will usually learn in fewer lessons than an older person. In fact most instructors will tell you that to obtain the standard of driving required to pass the test it will take at least one hour's lesson for every year of the pupil's life. People who play active sports, especially ball games, learn more quickly than academics. This is because their co-ordination is usually better at first. Practical people also usually learn to drive quite quickly because often being interested in mechanics they probably know or can more easily understand the workings of a car. Sex, that is, whether it is a male or female learning to drive does not make any difference. I know this last statement is contrary to popular opinion but in my experience I have found it to be true. A man and woman of equal age learn in a very similar way.

Does instruction technique differ when teaching the 'quick learner' or the 'slow learner'?

Not really. One of the problems is that you do not know whether a person is going to learn quickly or slowly until he or she has had a few lessons. You must always be aware that although a person might start to learn very quickly, showing great promise at first, this progress may then slow down or even grind almost to a halt at one stage before it all 'clicks' into place.

The only difference in teaching different people is the time that has to be taken on each point of learning before moving on to the next. You may have to go over something many more times with one person than with another. The way that you teach any particular problem does not differ. The really important point is that you are sure that the pupil has fully understood the particular manoeuvre that you have been teaching, however long it takes.

Problems for the instructor

Having discussed the relative time that it takes different people to learn to drive we now come to what is probably the most important point for the instructor.

Most amateur instructor/pupil relationships come to grief because the instructor tries to make the pupil do things that are quite impossible for a person of limited driving experience to attempt. It may be a manoeuvre such as turning a corner, or just the method in which something is taught.

Remember, just because you have done something that appears to be easy, in a certain way for many years, it might be an extremely difficult manoeuvre for the person you are teaching. You can probably think of certain things that you do in your own driving that you would not think of passing on to the pupil. The trouble is that these things are fairly obvious, and so although you make an effort to show the pupil the correct way to do these things, there are probably many other things that you do not realise could be far more dangerous to the learner. This is the whole essence of teaching somebody to drive. Everything must be done in the pupil's own time and must be done in the way and at the speed that the learner can do it. Not at the speed that you can do it!

The learner must be inspired with confidence. This can only be done if the pupil has confidence in you and your method of teaching. Always remember that some of the most simple things in driving to you, can be extremely difficult to the pupil. For example, take the seemingly easy manoeuvre of turning left into a side road while travelling down a hill. You have probably turned into such a turning thousands of times without having any problems. In fact, it is so easy to you by now that you have not even given a thought as to how exactly you accomplish this manoeuvre. You are astonished, therefore, when you tell the person you are teaching to do this same manoeuvre, that the result is a near catastrophe. You find that instead of taking the left turn smoothly, the pupil panics just before the turning and attempts it so fast that he nearly demolishes the brick wall on the other side of the road. This also causes you to panic and the mutual harmony and confidence that you tried to build up has been lost possibly for ever. Where did you go wrong?

Because of your inexperience as an instructor you did not realise the difficulties that the learner was going to encounter. All the left turns previously taken had been on the level or going up the hill and so when the clutch was pushed down to enable him to change gear, the car did not increase speed. But this time the car suddenly increased speed when the clutch was depressed. The pupil panicked and put his foot on the accelerator instead of the brake with the obvious result. An experienced instructor would have anticipated the danger and warned the pupil to brake more as he approached the turning to counteract the car gaining speed when the clutch was depressed and to be ready to keep his foot on the brake even as he started to turn the corner, making sure he was not still depressing the clutch while turning.

All very simple, once you know how! Remember some of the most difficult things are not obvious. Driving along a main road with a fair amount of traffic can be easier to the learner than taking a sharp left turn.

All through the book there will be notes on problems similar to this to enable them to be anticipated. Read the notes carefully because they are most important.

Always 'talk' the pupil through the correct procedures

In the first few lessons you will have to dictate everything to the pupil. This is very important because one of the vital aspects of learning to drive is that the pupil learns the procedure in the correct order for each manoeuvre by constant repetition and practice.

Whenever he moves off, for instance, the procedure is always the same, with possible slight variations depending upon the particular circumstances prevailing at the time. Until the pupil has had several lessons he will not be able to remember the correct routine for each manoeuvre. Therefore, it is up to you, as the instructor, to 'talk' him through every stage of every manoeuvre. Gradually, as the pupil improves, you can leave out some stages to allow him to use his own initiative but make certain that he still keeps to the correct routine. It is all too easy for the pupil to develop bad habits which can prove extremely difficult to correct later. An example of this is in his use of the mirror. If you do not continually remind him to look in the mirror before he gives a signal it will not be long before he is either not looking in the mirror at all or he will be using the mirror after he signals. In the later lessons you will not be 'talking' him through control procedures, except possibly some gear changing, but you will still be talking through road procedures and traffic situations.

Practise 'talking' the pupil through manoeuvres and procedures

You can practise 'talking' through manoeuvres while driving yourself, before you begin to teach the pupil to drive. Every time you drive you should go through, in your mind, every movement that you make because it is probably a very long time since you have actually thought about the technique of driving. As an experienced driver you react to situations on the road naturally, without having to think about the necessary individual movements with the controls. If you can now begin to think about this technique as you drive yourself it will be a great help when teaching.

The pupil must listen and follow your instruction

Make sure that the pupil listens to your instructions while he is driving and that he attempts to follow the instructions as precisely as he can, especially in the early lessons when he is likely to be very nervous and tense. This tenseness in the first few lessons can cause the pupil to give the impression that he is not listening to and obeying your instructions, whereas he is making every effort to do so. It is just that his limbs will not respond in the way that he wishes them to, or because of his inward state of panic, he will use one control when you are telling him to use another. The only answer to this problem is to tell him to relax and try to put him at his ease.

There is, however, the possibility that the pupil is actually not listening to you and as this can be a far more serious problem I will use up some space discussing it.

Very often the pupil tries to think too much for himself at first and instead of listening to your instructions he attempts to 'do it his own way'. For example, you will be telling him to brake slightly but he will respond by putting down the clutch, or you will tell him to look in the mirror but instead he will change gear. The only possible result of this situation is confusion. If it is allowed to continue, the pupil will learn nothing. It is vital in the first few lessons, that the pupil does not think for himself, while he is actually driving, but allows you to do the thinking for him. The pupil must concentrate on finding the position and response of the controls while at the same time going through the procedure of each manoeuvre by correctly obeying the instructions that you give him. He will find this quite enough to worry about without trying to think why he is doing it or what he is going to do next. (Once the car is stationary with the hand brake on and the gear in neutral, he can then think about the driving he has done and ask you any questions.) It will not be long before he can think for himself and listen to your instructions at the same time but he must learn and practise the basic technique of driving before this is possible. This can only be done by obeying your instructions and it is up to you to ensure that he listens and does his best to follow the correct procedures at all times.

Repetition

However, you should not worry that you have to keep repeating the same instructions every lesson. It is a different problem and quite normal for the pupil to continuously forget to look over his shoulder, or in the mirror, or to move into the correct position for a certain manoeuvre. This is unfortunately particularly true in later lessons when you will probably have hoped for better things. Just persevere with your reminders and eventually he will remember it all, or nearly all! This is where the patience and good humour of the driving instructor is really tested. I think that it is the problem of forgetfulness that is the most common of all when teaching somebody to drive well enough to pass a driving test.

Safety tips for the instructor

The tips given below will be helpful to you during your period as an instructor. Some of them are so important that they are stated again several times during the course. The repetition is quite intentional; they cannot be stressed enough because of their importance. It will be a good idea to read these 'tips for the instructor' before each lesson to keep them in your mind.

1. *Never take your eyes off the road for more than a second.* It is amazing how quickly a pupil can veer to the right or left. Even when travelling at relatively slow speed this can be extremely dangerous.
2. *Never become over-confident in the ability of the pupil.* When a pupil has progressed to the later stage of learning it is all too easy

for the instructor to lapse in concentration. This can be fatal because it must be remembered that the pupil is still very inexperienced. Watch for the following:

(a) *Freezing.* The term 'freezing' is used when the pupil suddenly becomes transfixed by a situation. It can happen at any time and in any circumstances; therefore, if the instructor is not aware of it then disaster can be the result. It usually affects braking and steering; the pupil can be heading into a dangerous situation, he knows it is dangerous, he knows he is going too fast but he does nothing about it. The instructor can be shouting at him to come off the accelerator, or brake, or turn the wheel but the pupil just continues with his foot depressing the accelerator. This is very common at the early stage of learning, and because it is expected, it can be easily dealt with. But watch for it all through the course because the more advanced the pupil the more dangerous it is. It is caused by nerves and tension but it affects some pupils more than others. The only remedy is to use the handbrake or turn the wheel yourself. This is why you must realise that it is happening to be able to act early enough.

(b) *When any hazard or danger is approaching always be ready to grasp the steering wheel and apply the brake.*

(c) *Act on your own suspicions.* If you have a feeling that the pupil is going too fast, is not in full control of the situation or is about to go too close to a stationary or moving vehicle, then he probably is, so tell him and be ready to act on it yourself. *Do not leave it too late.*

3. *Always look for yourself to see if it is safe to move away.* Do not rely on the pupil's judgement when he is moving off.

4. *Always try to act and sound relaxed.* Not easy, this one! There will be times when you feel anything but relaxed. It is important, however, to convey a feeling of confidence to the pupil, so do not become too jumpy or aggravated.

5. *Do not worry too much about other motorists becoming aggravated.* Sometimes other motorists become annoyed when they are following a learner. Although, of course, you should do your utmost not to cause inconvenience, there will be times when this will be unavoidable. If you become worried about the other motorists it will cause the pupil to start worrying which must be avoided if possible.

You will find plenty of comments and notes giving advice throughout the course and these will help you to overcome some of the problems that may arise later.

The First Lesson – Preparation

It is important to find the quietest roads possible for this lesson. Even if you live in a busy area, you can always find a convenient place within a mile or two of your home.

The ideal starting place is in a long side road with other roads leading off. In this first lesson there will be very little actual driving because most of the time will be spent explaining the controls. This lesson does not include turning at junctions but as you will be starting at the same place in the next two lessons, when turning at junctions will be taught, it is best if you can find a 'block' where you can keep turning left or right and finish back at the same place. Make sure that it does not entail your entering any busy roads. (See Fig. 1.)

It is not a good idea to use a large open space such as a car park or disused airfield. Although it appears to be the safest place it tends to give the learner a false impression of widths of the road. He has got to start on proper roads some time so it might as well be now.

Make sure that you are familiar with the layout of the roads before the lesson and watch out for any cul-de-sacs. There is nothing worse than driving up a dead-end.

Read the lesson before starting
Take your time reading the lesson yourself a few times before going out with the pupil. You should do this before you start any of the lessons. Make sure that the learner reads the lesson thoroughly.

Before going on the road make sure:
1. The learner has a Provisional Licence.
2. The car is insured.

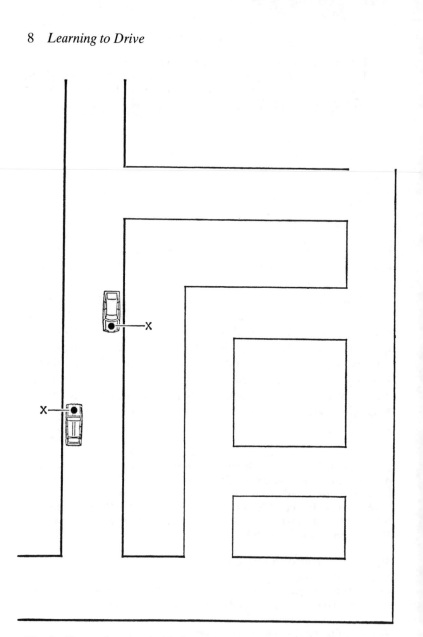

Fig. 1 Types of roads suitable for the first few lessons (start at either of the points marked with X).

3. That 'L' plates are fixed to front and rear of car.
4. The learner's eyesight is up to the requirements of the driving test. (i.e. He should be able to read a number plate from 23 metres (25 yards).)

The First Lesson – Practice

Duration of lesson approximately one hour

Drive your pupil to your starting place, making sure that you are on the level. Park the car, switch off the engine and change places with the pupil. It is important that he is sitting in the driving seat so that he can get the feel of the controls while you are explaining them to him.

You are now going to explain the controls of the car and later practise them with him before moving off.

Controls

Panel and dashboard
The only thing to concern you at this stage is the ignition key. When it is turned to this position the ignition is switched on. Then turn it more and the engine starts. As soon as the engine fires take your hand off the key.

Practise it a couple of times. It is not worth running through all the other switches such as lights, windscreen wipers, etc. at this stage, as long as you are conversant with them before you take your test.

Gears
There are four or sometimes five forward gears and one reverse. The four forward gears are in the same position in virtually all cars. They are in the shape of the letter 'H'. (See Fig. 2.)

Hold the gear lever firmly but not too tightly. It is important to be as relaxed as possible. Now run through the forward gears. Feel the movement in neutral, then place into 1st, 2nd, 3rd and 4th. Then back into 3rd, 2nd, 1st and neutral. Ignore 5th gear, if fitted, at this stage.

Make sure that you are holding the gear lever properly. There is no hard and fast rule as to the correct way of holding it as long as it is natural. For some gear levers it is best to use the palm of the hand to slide it into gear, some it is best to grip the lever with the fingers. You must decide the best way to hold the gears.

If the gears on your car are on the steering wheel you must adapt your instructions for this.

Practise running through the gears for a few moments, especially the movement from 2nd to 3rd and *vice versa*, and 4th to 2nd. It is not necessary to depress the clutch to practise the gear change when the engine is not running but in some cars the gears may be easier to handle if the clutch is depressed. Do not worry about reverse gear at this stage. You have enough to think about with the other four.

If you are having a lot of trouble with the gear change leave it for now. You can always practise it in your spare time.

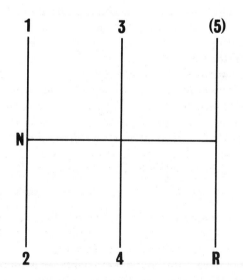

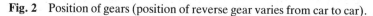

Fig. 2   Position of gears (position of reverse gear varies from car to car).

Hand brake

The hand brake is in the 'on' position at the moment. In other words it is up. To release the hand brake you must first lift it slightly and with your thumb depress the button. When it is right down take your hand off the hand brake.

When lifting the hand brake the button must again be depressed until the hand brake is as high as possible. Then, keeping the hand brake up, release the button.

Practise releasing and applying the hand brake several times. You may have trouble in pressing the button in at the right time, especially when releasing the hand brake. It is usually because you have not lifted it enough. Although it is a relatively simple control it is quite surprising the trouble that it can cause at first until you have got the knack of it. (The reason that you are taught to press the button in when the hand brake is applied is to avoid damaging the ratchet.)

Indicators
(If on the right of the steering wheel)

When you want to indicate that you are turning left you put the indicator up and when you want to indicate right, put the indicator down. Try and operate the indicator with one finger, without taking your hand off the steering wheel.

There is a light which flashes to warn you that you are indicating. Although they usually cancel themselves, there will be occasions when they do not, so always check the warning light and, if necessary cancel it. (If the indicator switch is on the left of the steering wheel then left would be down and right would be up.)

The best way to explain the up and down position to the pupil is to compare it with the direction of the steering wheel. When the wheel is going to be turned to the left, then the indicator is turned in the same direction.

If the indicators are not on the steering wheel, then adapt your instructions accordingly.

Foot pedals

There are three pedals. From right to left they are accelerator, brake and clutch (CBA).

The accelerator and brake are used with your right foot, the clutch with the left. Never use anything else with your left foot apart from the clutch.

Time must now be taken to explain each pedal in detail.

Accelerator (or gas pedal or throttle) (also see page 29)
When the engine is running, pressure on the accelerator pedal increases the amount of petrol that is sucked into the engine. This increases the speed of the engine and, when moving, the speed of the car. When the pressure is lifted from the accelerator, the amount of petrol being pumped into the engine decreases and therefore the car slows down. In fact, the action of lifting the pressure off the accelerator acts as a brake on the car. It will not slow the car down very much but at least it helps.

Remember, if you take your foot right off the accelerator the engine will not stop.

This point often confuses pupils. It is important to understand that the engine will 'idle' on its own without pressure on the accelerator.

Foot brake (see also page 40)
Always use the foot brake for slowing down or stopping, never the hand brake. (The hand brake is only used when the car is stationary.)

It will take some time to get used to the feel of the accelerator and brake pedals. They should both be used very gently at first.

Most learners have a lot of trouble controlling both the brake and accelerator pedals at first. Practise on the accelerator for a few minutes after the rest of the controls have been explained.

Clutch
Because of its importance, it is well worth spending some minutes explaining the way that the clutch works, when it is used and why.

It is realised that the learner is probably not mechanically minded, but the following method of explaining it is usually successful. It is vital that at least some understanding of the clutch is achieved at this stage. The whole basis of driving hinges on this.

Most people have ridden a bicycle at some stage of their life. If they have not ridden one they have certainly seen one.

On a bicycle is a chain. This chain connects the pedals with the back wheel. When the pedals are turned the chain is pushed round and therefore the back wheel also turns. In other words, the power (i.e. the rider of the bike) turns the pedals, the pedals turn the chain, the chain turns the back, or drive wheel and the bicycle moves.

If the chain breaks or comes off there is no connection between the pedals and the wheel and so the bicycle can no longer be powered.

The same can be applied to a car. Imagine now that we have started the engine. It does not matter how fast the engine is running, how hard you put your foot on the accelerator, because until we connect the engine to the drive wheels it will never move the car.

On a car it is impracticable to use a chain, so another method is used. It is done with gears.

Connected to the gear lever is a small wheel with cogs. This wheel is connected to the drive wheels of the car. Connected to the engine are four other wheels which are called gears. They also have cogs on. So gears are only small wheels of varying sizes all with cogs or 'teeth'.

If, by pushing the gear lever into 1st gear, you connect the small wheel on the end of the gear lever with one of the gear wheels that are connected to the engine, you have then connected the engine to the drive wheels of the car. This is what is meant by the expression 'putting it into gear'.

To disconnect the engine from the back wheels you just pull the gear lever back into neutral. This separates the gear wheels from the wheel on the end of the gear lever and there is now a gap between the engine and the drive wheels. 'Neutral' means that no gear is connected and therefore the engine is free to turn on its own. If a gear is selected and the engine turned on, the car would jump forward. When in neutral the engine can be started without causing the car to move forward.

What has all this got to do with the clutch? Everything!

Up until now we have explained how to connect the engine to the drive wheels while the engine is not running. What happens when the engine is running? Problems!

As soon as the engine is running the gear wheels which, remember, are joined to the engine, start turning. The more you put your foot on the accelerator, the faster the engine runs and the faster the gear wheels turn. It is now impossible to connect the stationary wheel that is connected to the gear lever with the turning wheel. If you did try it a terrible scraping noise would occur when the stationary wheel and moving wheel touched.

So somehow you have to stop the gear wheel from turning, even though the engine is running. This is where the clutch comes in.

Between the engine and the gears are two metal discs. One is joined to the engine, the other to the gears. Normally these metal discs are pressed together but when you push the clutch pedal down these two metal discs separate. The one that is connected to the engine continues to turn. The other stops turning. As this disc is connected to the gears, they also stop turning. So once you have put your foot down on the clutch pedal it is possible to join any one of the gears to the back wheel by placing the gear lever into the gear selected. Now all that needs to be done is for you to lift the clutch by raising your foot. This will connect the two metal discs. The disc joined to the engine will start turning the other disc which is connected to the gears. The gears will turn, the back wheels will turn and the car will start moving. (See Fig. 3.)

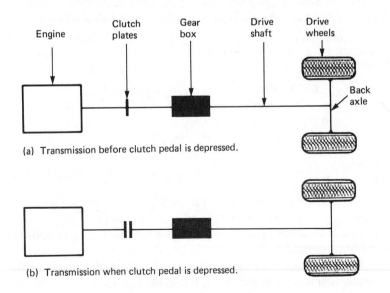

(a) Transmission before clutch pedal is depressed.

(b) Transmission when clutch pedal is depressed.

Fig. 3 How the clutch works.

To move the car, therefore, all you have to do is switch the engine on, push the clutch down, put the gear lever into gear and lift your foot off the clutch? Not quite!

It is the way you lift the clutch when you move off from a stationary position that is so important. Remember that the car is a heavy piece of machinery, and that the engine is running, but the back wheels are stationary. When the engine connects with the back wheels there is a lot of friction at the point at which they meet. This is where the two metal discs come together and is called the 'biting point', or point of contact. It is this biting point that is so vital to the control of the car. In fact, when you want to move off from a stationary position, the clutch must only be lifted to this biting point and not further. If the clutch is lifted too far, then the car will jump forward in a series of 'kangaroo jumps' or the engine will stop. This is called stalling. This biting point is usually about halfway between the clutch being fully depressed and fully up. Its position can differ from car to car, so do not always expect it to be in the same place in all cars.

When the clutch has reached the 'biting point', you must hold it there while the car begins to pull away. Once the car has moved a few yards the clutch pedal can be gently released altogether.

The importance of holding the clutch at the 'biting' point is often not realised by experienced drivers. It is very important to stress this point.

When you watch other people drive, it may appear that they are not holding the 'biting point' on the clutch. They are! It is just that they have used the clutch so many thousands of times that they know exactly how long to hold it so that the car will move off smoothly. This will take you quite a long time to master, but eventually you will be doing it as quickly as they do. The more slowly you do it at first, the better.

The clutch is then used every time you change gear. When the car is moving it is not necessary to be so exact in lifting the clutch. It can be lifted reasonably quickly as long as it is brought up evenly and not suddenly snatched off.

The only other time the clutch is used is when you stop the car. Remember it is the brake that will stop the car. In other words, the clutch has nothing to do with slowing the car, but if you did not push the clutch down just before you stopped, the engine would stall.

This is because the car is in gear when you stop. Therefore the engine is connected to the back wheels, so that when the wheels stopped turning the engine would stop. To avoid this happening, you must depress the clutch so that the two metal discs are apart, and the engine can keep running even though the rest of the car is stationary. The clutch must be kept down until the gear lever is returned to neutral.

So the only times that you use the clutch are when you want to select a gear (this includes moving off from a stationary position) and when you stop. Never put the clutch down at any other time because the car is then 'free wheeling' or 'coasting'. This can be very dangerous, because the car can increase speed when you depress the clutch when going downhill, and you would have less control. It is therefore, especially dangerous to 'free-wheel' downhill.

There has been no mention at this stage of the use of the accelerator when moving away. It would only confuse the pupil at this stage. It will be fully covered when we come to actually moving off.

Steering

You should hold the steering wheel in the 'ten to two' position on a clock (i.e. both hands parallel just above the centre of the wheel).

Some people have a lot of trouble with the steering at first. One of the reasons is that they do not look far enough ahead when driving. Never look at, or just beyond, the bonnet of the car, or at the kerb, as this will cause you to wander. Always look well ahead along the road. Do not grip the steering wheel too tightly. At first you will be nervous and tense which usually results in gripping the wheel too tightly, relax them off the wheel and this will help you to relax.

Never cross your hands over each other when cornering. In fact, each hand should always stay on the correct side of the wheel. This method of turning the wheel is called the 'push and pull method'. In other words, if you are turning to the left, make sure that the left hand pulls down until it has reached nearly the bottom of the wheel and the right hand pushes up until it reaches near the top. The left hand should then be removed from the wheel and placed near the top. When this is done, the right hand can be placed near the bottom to start the turn again. BOTH HANDS MUST NEVER LEAVE THE WHEEL SIMULTANEOUSLY WHEN YOU ARE TURNING.

Remember when you are driving along a fairly straight road very little steering is needed, but when cornering or manoeuvring the wheel has to be turned many times in the correct manner (i.e. without crossing your hands). This is an important point because most learners tend to over-steer when driving down fairly straight roads and understeer when going round corners.

Don't forget to straighten the wheel after going round the corner. You should use the push and pull method when straightening up.

Always try to glance at the pupil's eyes in the early lessons to check that he is looking in the correct place. This is especially important when the pupil is straightening up the car after negotiating a sharp bend or corner. Try to make the pupil look in the direction that the car should finish after taking the corner. The same applies when passing parked vehicles. Very often the pupil tends to look at the vehicle, and therefore drives into or much too close to it.

In the early lessons you must be very alert to the pupil's steering problems. Some have great difficulty at first, especially in judging how much to turn the wheel, and nearly all pupils forget to straighten the wheel after negotiating a corner. This can be particularly dangerous if the pupil accelerates before straightening the wheel. You must be ready at any time to grab the wheel. This does not mean, however, that you must continuously have your hand a few inches from the wheel as this would be off-putting to the pupil.

When you grab the wheel always aim to hold it at the lower half, (somewhere around the seven or eight position of a clock face). You can then go under the arm of the pupil, thereby avoiding your hand getting mixed up with his hand. It is well worth practising this a few times before you start so that you can be confident of being able to judge the distance of the wheel in an emergency. There is nothing worse than misjudging the distance and instead of grabbing the wheel, missing it altogether. You only get one chance in an emergency.

Procedure before starting the engine

Adjust seat

It is essential to be sitting in a comfortable position. Adjust the seat so as to be able to reach the pedals easily. If you can depress the clutch right down to the floor with your knee still slightly bent, you are correct in your position. If you can adjust the height of the seat, make sure that you are as high as possible and comfortable. You can always use a cushion to gain height.

Seat belt
Always wear your seat belt from the beginning, as this will enable you to get used to it as soon as possible. Make sure it is comfortable and adjusted properly.

Mirror
Once you are in the correct seated position you can now adjust the mirror. Make sure that you have the clearest view possible out of the back window. Remember that the mirror is vitally important. You must use it BEFORE you signal, change direction, pull out, turn, slow down and stop. In fact, you use it before you do anything. You should also look in your mirror occasionally when you are driving on a straight road so that you know the situation behind.

Two important points about the mirror:

1. When you move off from a stationary position at the side of the road it is not sufficient just to look in the mirror. You can only see directly out of the back of the car in the mirror, therefore, there is a blind spot to your off-side. You must always look over your right shoulder before you decide it is safe to pull away. Even if the car is fitted with wing mirrors, it is still probable that there is a blind spot somewhere behind you where a cyclist could be, so always look round.
2. Always glance in the mirror for less than a second. This is not easy at first, because it is difficult to take in what is happening behind you as quickly as that. Distances are difficult to judge at first when looking in the mirror, but it will become easier with practice.

    It is easy to find yourself looking in the mirror for two or three seconds and when you look out to the front again discover that you are driving towards a lamp post or a car travelling in the opposite direction. In fact, if you take your eyes off the road at all, only do it for a split second.

That goes equally for the instructor. NEVER TAKE YOUR EYES OFF THE ROAD FOR MORE THAN A SPLIT SECOND.

Hand brake and gear lever
Make sure the hand brake is in the 'on' position and that the gear lever is in neutral.

The above procedure should always be carried out when you first get into the car. It can be done in a short time once the correct procedure is firmly in your mind.

Remember, if you stall the engine, which you are bound to do, always put the hand brake on and put the gear lever into neutral before you restart the engine. It is better always to have the gear lever in neutral before you start the engine. If the engine is stalled it allows a few seconds to collect your thoughts before starting the engine. If the clutch is depressed with the car in gear while you start the engine you will probably stall it again and panic.

Check all doors are properly closed
There is just one other thing before you start the engine. MAKE SURE the doors are all shut. It sounds obvious but can be disastrous if overlooked.

You can now tell the pupil to start the engine.

Once the engine is going, depress the accelerator very slightly. It is vital to listen to the sound of the engine at different engine speeds. Make sure that your heel is on the floor and that your foot is in a comfortable position. At first you will tend to hold your foot very tense and this is often a cause of cramp or discomfort in the shin. A comfortable sitting position will help this.

It is important to impress on the pupil the sound that the engine makes for different needs, e.g. purring sound for moving away on the level, slightly more for starting on a hill, more still for starting on a very steep hill and so on.

Also practise lifting your foot from the pedal, without taking it right away, and then putting pressure on the pedal again. Very often you will think your foot is right up from the accelerator when in fact you are still accelerating slightly. This can cause problems later so practise it. Then practise moving your right foot from the accelerator on to the brake and back again a few times, so that you get the feeling of where they are in relation to each other. Make sure you do not look at your feet.

Impress upon him that gentle movements on the accelerator and brake are essential for a smooth ride, especially when travelling in low gear.

Let the pupil run through the forward four gears once more (this time with the clutch depressed of course). When you are satisfied that he has got the feeling of the gears you are ready for moving off.

We are now going to move away. The procedure for moving away is always the same (except when moving off down a hill, this will be explained later).

Make sure you teach him to move away with the same procedure each time.

Moving off on the level

1. Depress clutch.
   Whenever the clutch is depressed, make sure that it is pressed right down to the floor. In fact try and press the clutch through the floor then you know that it is right down. Also remember that the quicker you push the clutch down, the better. (It is when you lift it that you have to be gentle.)
2. Select 1st gear.
3. Find the correct amount of acceleration (purring sound) and keep it in that position all the time.
4. Lift the clutch slowly until you hear the engine change sound, when you will also feel a slight movement of the car. (This is the 'biting point'.) Hold the clutch in this position.
5. Look in the rear-view mirror and over your right shoulder.
6. Give a right signal, with the indicator, if necessary (i.e. if it would help any other road users including pedestrians). If the road is clear and it is safe (look round again) . . .
7. Release the hand brake – replacing your hand on the steering wheel immediately.
8. Start lifting the clutch slowly until you feel the car beginning to pull away. As soon as it begins to move, hold your foot at that position on the clutch, making sure that you keep your other foot steady on the accelerator.

There is no need for you to increase pressure on the accelerator at this stage. It is far better to concentrate on the movement of your left foot on the clutch.

Stages 7 and 8 can be performed simultaneously with more practice.

Once the car has moved off you must keep the clutch in the same position until the car has gone three or four metres (yards) then gently release the rest of the clutch by gently lifting off your foot. At the same time you can increase pressure on the accelerator very slightly.

Now that the clutch has been released completely the accelerator alone will alter the speed of the car, but keep your left foot near the clutch in case you need it.

Make sure that you are looking well ahead and relax those hands on the steering wheel.

Let the pupil control the car on his own for about 50 metres (55 yards) or so at a low steady speed, you should just be uttering words of encouragement. You may have to adjust his steering slightly at first, especially if there are obstacles (parked cars, skips, etc.), to negotiate. (Make a mental note of any obstructions or hazards before starting.)

Faults to look for

The most common faults when moving off are:

(*a*) Suddenly snatching the clutch off as the car makes its first movement.

(*b*) Lifting the foot from the accelerator as the clutch comes to the 'biting point'.

Only practice can cure these faults and in the next lesson these points will be explained and practised in more detail when you come to the hill start.

Two extra tips
1. Always make sure that as the pupil starts moving off you look in the mirror and look round yourself to make sure that it is safe to do so. Quite a few seconds would probably have elapsed since the pupil looked because at first he will be slow at moving away.
2. You should keep your feet near the pedals at all times in the early lessons. The left foot should be just over or adjacent to the

clutch and the right foot should be either over the accelerator or brake when they are not being used.

After some 50 to 75 metres (55 to 82 yards), tell the pupil that you want him to stop on the left. (Of course, everything at this stage must be dictated to the pupil.)

Stopping

Still with your foot gently on the accelerator and keeping both hands on the wheel:

1. *Look in the mirror.*
2. *If there is somebody behind you give a signal that you intend to stop. (Either an arm signal (explanation on page 25) or a left indicator.)*
3. *Lift right foot off accelerator and place over the brake, but do not press on the brake.*

As the car is travelling at a very slow speed in first gear the act of taking your foot off the accelerator will slow the car down very quickly. It is important, however, that you get the feeling of taking your foot off the accelerator and placing it over the brake while the car is moving, as long as the brake is not depressed unless needed, and then only gently.

4. *Depress clutch and, if needed, push down gently on brake. KEEP BOTH HANDS ON THE WHEEL.*

By this time the pupil should have steered into a reasonable parking position but a little help on the steering from you may be needed.

Once the car has stopped keep both feet down.
5. *Hand brake on. (Remember to press the button in.)*
6. *Gear into neutral.*
7. *Remove both feet from the pedals.*

Explain the seven points of stopping, especially the importance of normally braking before declutching. This always causes some confusion at first because at the very slow speed at which he will be travelling in this first lesson the car will almost stop without any brake being applied. Explain that this is the exception. Normally the brake will be needed to slow the car down before the clutch is used. (Also see page 41.)

Now we will move off again.

Go through exactly the same procedure as before when moving off. Do not expect any improvement, or for it to be accomplished any quicker.

Again, each stage must be dictated.

Once he has moved away and a reasonable speed attained, second gear can be engaged.

Changing gear

1. *Press the clutch right down to the floor (as quickly as possible) and at the same time lift the right foot off the accelerator. Just keep your right foot over the accelerator otherwise you will not be able to find it again.*

2. *Shift the gear from 1st into 2nd. Do not look at the gears. Do it slowly and evenly.*

A little guidance with your hand on the lower part (stem) of the gear lever may be needed.

3. *Lift the clutch gently, depressing the accelerator at the same time.*

Co-ordination is the important thing here. Do not expect to time the clutch and accelerator movements perfectly at first. There will be plenty of time to get this right later.

The only important thing is that you do not snatch your foot too quickly off the clutch or go too hard down on the accelerator.

Give the pupil a chance to get the feel of the accelerator with the car in second gear. Explain that more speed is now possible with less effort. If there is still quite a lot of reasonably straight road available then 3rd gear can be engaged. Exactly the same procedure as for 2nd gear but ensure that he has enough speed to change into 3rd. Remember the pupil must change the gear slowly so allow enough speed for the car to slow down. You will almost certainly have to help to guide the gear into 3rd as this is a more difficult movement for him. Make sure he does not look down at the gears because this is a very difficult habit to break later.

Once in 3rd gear let the pupil get the feel of the accelerator and power of the car in that gear. Make sure he does not go too fast though.

If you considered that there was not enough road for 3rd gear then let him stay in 2nd. It does not matter which gear the pupil stops in. If in 3rd stay in 3rd, if in 2nd stay in 2nd.

Tell the pupil to stop in a parking position on the left. Talk him through the seven points on stopping and make sure that he does them as you say them. Do not push him into the next point before he has completed the previous one.

Once stopped explain any point which you consider needs elaboration. By now he should be getting into his mind the procedures for moving off, stopping and changing gear.

Impress on him that these procedures are always the same.

This is a good opportunity to explain to the pupil that it does not matter what gear is engaged when the car stops. There is a popular misconception that a pupil must always engage 2nd gear for stopping. This is quite wrong.

The only reason that you change down to 2nd gear before stopping is if there is a possibility of continuing on without actually stopping (e.g. when approaching a junction where it could be possible to see that the road was clear, and therefore where you would be able to continue at a slow speed for which 2nd gear would be essential).

Approaching pedestrian crossings and traffic lights could be the same because they could become clear of pedestrians or change to green just as you approached and you could then continue without actually stopping. To do this in 3rd gear would probably be impossible.

If, however, you are stopping where there is no possibility of your continuing, for example when parking, then it is better to stay in whichever gear you were in. At least then you can keep both hands on the wheel.

This is also a good time to explain the use of signals when stopping, as this can also cause confusion to the learner.

Signals when stopping

There are two possible signals that you can give before stopping:

1. Arm signal. This is the up and down signal given with your right arm extended as far as possible out of the window. When possible you should always give this signal when you are slowing down or stopping.
2. Left indicator. Great care must be exercised when using the left indicator signal for stopping because it can cause confusion to other motorists and pedestrians. Remember, using the left indicator can also mean that you are turning left or that you are

pulling in to the left. If you are near a junction it is particularly dangerous to give a left indicator signal to show that you are stopping, because both following traffic and traffic emerging from the junction may think that you are turning left. The results could be disastrous.

There are times when you cannot possibly use the left indicator signal for stopping, such as at pedestrian crossings. You must use the arm signal for this. It is important to remember that by giving a slowing down (or stopping) arm signal at pedestrian crossings you are not only telling the vehicles behind you that you intend to stop but you are also telling pedestrians waiting to cross your intentions.

Other arm signals

You should know how to use all of the arm signals (i.e. left, right and stopping).

Although the stopping signal is used more frequently than the other two arm signals, there are times when the right and left signals could be important. The right arm signal, for instance, would be useful to show your intention to turn right into a side road if you had just given a right indication to show that you were pulling out from a parked car.

Other road users, for example motorcyclists, have to use arm signals, therefore to enable you to understand their intentions it is important that you are familiar with all these signals.

Show the pupil the three arm signals and let him practise them for a few minutes. Make sure that when the right and left arm signals are practised, the palm of the hand faces forward. For the stopping signal the palm should be facing down.
You should make the following point while on the subject of signalling.

Signalling in general (also see page 32)

All signals (both with indicators or arm) are given to tell other road users of your intentions; not to tell other road users what they should do. In other words when you give a left signal it means 'I am turning left or pulling in'. A right signal means 'I am turning right or pulling over to the right', and the up and down arm signal means 'I am slowing down or stopping'. It does not mean that 'because I am slowing down or stopping, you must stop too'. What the person behind does after you have given your signal is up to him. You should also make sure, after you have given your signal, that the other driver has acted in the correct way.

If you are turning right for instance, do not presume that the person behind you will not still try to overtake you, even after you have given the right signal.

You should never give signals to pedestrians that could endanger them. Never wave pedestrians across the road, even at pedestrian crossings. You must leave the decision to cross to them.

It is best to finish the lesson at this point because you do not want to over-tire the pupil on his first lesson.

The Second Lesson – Preparation

In the first lesson you have been shown the controls of the car, and the workings of the clutch were explained. You may not have fully understood the explanation of the clutch then, but you now have an opportunity, before the next lesson, to read the passage through, several times if necessary. You should also read the rest of Lesson 1 as a form of revision immediately before you start Lesson 2.

In the next lesson you will be negotiating corners for the first time. Before the lesson you should read the following notes so that you have some knowledge of bends and road junctions. Then you should read the advice on braking on page 40.

You should refer to these again after you have had a few more lessons, especially if you are experiencing any difficulties at corners.

Corners
So far you have only had to drive on a straight road but even then you probably found some difficulty in keeping the car on the course that you wanted. It takes a little while to know how the car will respond when the steering wheel is turned, but provided that you obey the advice given in Lesson 1 (i.e. looking well ahead, holding the wheel in the correct place and relaxing as much as possible) you will soon get the feel of it.

When you steer round corners you will have far greater problems to contend with because, apart from the fact that you will have to judge how much to turn the wheel, you will also have to take into account the speed of your car, the gradients you are on and the type of corner that it is.

Speed at corners (use of acceleration)

The car should be at its lowest speed at the moment you begin to turn the corner and you must be 'driving' the vehicle while you continue and complete the turn. The term 'driving' in this context means that the car must be controlled by the engine. To be able to do this it is essential to be in a very low gear to give you the control that is needed at such a slow speed. You must also have your foot off the clutch (not 'riding' the clutch).

How slowly, and which low gear you engage, will depend on how sharp and what type of corner it is. The sharper the corner, the slower the speed and the lower the gear. The amount of acceleration needed also varies because although you should not gain speed as you are turning it might be necessary to accelerate slightly to keep the car moving, especially if you are on an incline. In this context you can see that 'to accelerate' does not necessarily mean 'to increase speed' because you may need to accelerate to remain at the same speed.

Having turned a sharp corner remember that you still need to straighten the car, so be careful not to increase speed until you have done this. On wider corners you can increase speed slightly as you come out of the corner.

Corners really come under two basic categories. These are bends, which we have just discussed, and junctions which we will now discuss in detail.

Junctions

Although the same principles apply to junctions as apply to bends regarding your speed and position on approach, you have the added problem of more than one road to deal with at junctions.

The layout of junctions can vary considerably from the usual 'T' shaped junction to a complicated intersection of trunk roads like 'Spaghetti junction'. At first you must become accustomed to the more simple type but as you progress to the more difficult type of junctions you will find that the following instructions will only have to be adapted slightly because basically the same rules and procedure apply to them all.

Approach to junctions (See Fig. 4)

MIRROR – SIGNAL – MANOEUVRE (MSM)

When you are approaching junctions the MSM routine is vitally important to your own and other people's safety. I will break down each part of the routine to explain in detail just how important each stage is and why the procedure must be done in the correct order.

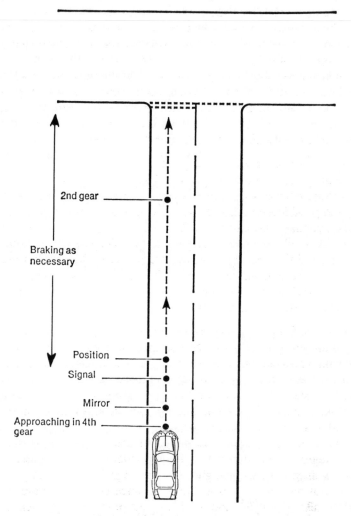

2nd gear

Braking as necessary

Position

Signal

Mirror

Approaching in 4th gear

Fig. 4 Approaching a 'T' junction.

Mirror

In the first lesson it was stressed how important it is to look in the mirror before any manoeuvre is attempted. You will have noticed that when you practised the procedure for moving off you looked both in the mirror, and over your right shoulder, immediately before moving forward. When you were told to stop the first thing that you did was look in the mirror. It is vital then that you look in the mirror at the correct time for maximum safety because you must be aware of exactly what is happening behind you immediately BEFORE you attempt any manoeuvre.

When you are approaching a junction, whether you are going to turn left, right or if it is crossroads and you are going straight on, you must, before anything else, use your mirror to check the situation behind. You can then decide if it is safe to give the appropriate signal before continuing with the rest of the manoeuvre.

What to look for if you are turning left:
If you are going to turn left at the junction, you must check in your mirror for motor or pedal cyclists who could be travelling faster than you and possibly about to overtake you on your nearside (left). Of course, you must also look for other vehicles, especially if you are on a wide road, who could be trying to overtake you on your left. This can easily happen on a one-way street where other vehicles are allowed to overtake on the left. On other roads you would have to be rather too far out in the road for a large vehicle to try to overtake you on the nearside but it is possible.

What to look for if you are turning right:
If you are going to turn right the dangers are more obvious. It is quite likely that another vehicle is going to try to overtake you at the moment that you are about to signal and move out. Before you signal you must allow another vehicle to pass you if it is in the act of overtaking you or if you think that it is approaching at a fast speed behind you and therefore is obviously about to overtake. It is difficult to judge this when you are inexperienced but with practice your judgement will improve. When the other vehicle has passed, and it is then safe, you can give the right signal and change your position as necessary. This is the importance of using the mirror early to allow yourself time to delay your other actions, such as signalling and changing position, until it is safe to do so.

If you are not sure if the person following you is about to overtake then you should look in the mirror, wait a second then look in the mirror again. If he still does not look as though he is going to overtake then give the right signal, wait another second to check again in the mirror to ensure that you know his intentions before changing position yourself. Make sure that you are watching where you are going, so remember it must be quick glances in the mirror, not one long look.

What to look for when going straight on at crossroads:
You must use the mirror to decide if a slowing down arm signal is needed and to see if it is safe to adopt your correct position. You should look out for vehicles trying to overtake you on the nearside, especially if you are too far out towards the middle of the road as you approach.

Signal
Having decided, by using the mirror, that it is safe, you must then give the appropriate signal in good time. You should be careful about the timing of your signal because although normally you should give the signal as early as possible, you must also look out for other side roads before the one that you are going to take. You could mislead other road users into thinking that you are going to turn earlier than you intend to. This can be particularly dangerous when turning left, especially if there is another vehicle waiting to emerge from an earlier side road. If there is another side road before the turning you intend to take, you must wait until you have reached the first side road before you signal.

If you are going straight on at a crossroad you should give a slowing down arm signal if there is a vehicle following closely behind you.

You would never give a slowing down arm signal if you are turning right or left because, when you have indicated your intention to turn, other road users would expect you to slow down as you approached the corner. To give a slowing down signal would only confuse other drivers.

The important thing to remember as you approach any junction is that you must never change position in the road until you have checked in the mirror to see if it is safe and then given the appropriate signal.

Manoeuvre
You have now looked in your mirror and, having decided it is safe, given the correct signal. You are now ready for the manoeuvre. This can also be broken down into three separate items, i.e. **Position, Speed, Look (PSL).**

(*a*) *Position*
   You must get into the best position for approaching the junction as early as possible after having used your mirror and given the correct signal. The correct position will depend on which direction you are intending to turn.
   (*i*) *Turning left.*   You should already be on the left of your side of the road so there should be very little change of position necessary. There could, however, be an obstruction, e.g. a parked car on the left as you approach the junction, which would mean that you would have to be further out to avoid becoming trapped behind it. It is important that you see any obstruction early to allow you time to move out. There is nothing worse than having to suddenly swing out immediately before you turn left.
   You should normally approach the left turn about one metre (3 to 4 feet) from the kerb to allow enough room to negotiate the corner without either hitting the kerb as you turn or going too far out from the kerb as you enter the other road.
   (*ii*) *Turning right.*   You will have to move out into a position which is just to the left of the centre of the road (crown of the road) or, if there are lanes, into the correct lane. On narrow roads be careful not to go out too far to the right, especially if there are no white lines to guide you. Always move out smoothly, do not swing out into the middle of the road. When you reach the corner you must not endanger or inconvenience other road users by cutting off the corner or by stopping too far to the right of the road.
   (*iii*) *Straight on* (*crossroads*).   Adopt a similar position as when turning left unless the road markings or signs dictate otherwise.
   It is important, whichever way you are turning, to get into the correct position as early as possible and to stay in that position, without 'drifting' in or out. Remember that other vehicles will

probably start to overtake you once you have given your signal and adopted your position so any movement in or out at that stage can be very dangerous.

(*b*) *Speed*

You can now adjust your speed as necessary. This will mean braking and changing down the gears to enable you to approach the junction at the correct speed. By the time you reach the junction you should be travelling at a very slow speed so that you can either stop if necessary or continue on safely and under control. Most of the slowing down must be done with the brake because although the gears can help you to slow the car in certain circumstances (see page 61), it is the brake that you must rely on.

Sequence for slowing down when approaching junctions

Travelling at about 28 mph in 4th (or 3rd) gear at least 90 metres (100 yards) from turning:

1. Brake slightly, progressively slowing the car.

When the car is about 20 metres (23 yards) from the junction at a speed of about 10 mph.

2. Depress clutch and change down to 2nd gear (still braking as necessary).
3. Lift foot off clutch gently.

You should now be almost at the junction, travelling at 5 mph or less and ready to stop or turn as necessary.

From the above sequence you can see that you must brake almost continuously throughout the approach to the junction. You must judge the braking according to the circumstances (e.g. if you were going up hill you would need less braking than if you were on the flat. If you were approaching down a hill then you would need considerably more braking). It is difficult to judge the braking at first and sometimes you will find that you will have to adjust your braking as you approach because you have braked too hard or not hard enough. (For more information on braking see page 40.)

It is a common fault, when learning, to release the brake while you are changing down gear as you approach a junction. You must not do this because when the clutch is depressed the engine is not helping to slow the car therefore you must keep braking to counteract this, unless you are on an incline when the car would slow down even with the clutch depressed.

Another fault is that the right foot comes off the brake when the left foot comes off the clutch after changing gear. This is usually a subconscious movement of both feet working together.

One other important point concerning the above procedure is that the clutch must be lifted immediately after you have changed into the lower gear. You must not keep your foot depressing the clutch any longer than is necessary to change the gear because you would be 'coasting'. This means that you would not be controlling the car with the engine. It is a common fault, when learning to drive, to keep the clutch depressed after changing down gear.

When you reach the junction you must be ready to depress the clutch if you stop but if it is possible to continue on without stopping, then keep your foot over the clutch but not depressing it. At some junctions it might be advisable to change down to first gear as you approach to enable you to negotiate the turn at a very slow speed. You should not do this for the first few lessons, but, when you do, the technique is the same as for changing into the other gears but you must be moving at a very slow speed (about 5 mph).

One last point on braking. It is preferable to brake slightly too much when you are inexperienced at approaching junctions because it is safer and easier to lift your foot slightly off the brake pedal if you have slowed the car too much than it is to brake hard at the last moment, especially when approaching a junction while travelling downhill.

(c) *Looking*

Having approached the junction, in the correct position and at the proper speed, you now have to look to see if it is safe to continue into the other road.

How you look and what you look for will depend on the type of junction and whether you are turning right or left into a side road or into a main road.

1.   *Turning right into a side road*
   (*a*)   Look for oncoming traffic.
          If there is any traffic coming in the opposite direction as you
          approach the turning you must stop in the correct position
          (i.e. with the front of your car level with the centre of the
          road into which you are turning). When the road is clear of
          approaching traffic you can then enter the road.
          If there is no oncoming traffic as you approach the side
          road you can continue without stopping if it is safe to do so,
          making sure that you keep in the correct position as you
          turn (i.e. when the front of the car reaches the centre of the
          road into which you are turning, and not cutting off the
          corner, see Fig 7).
   (*b*)   Look into the road into which you are turning to make sure
          it is safe to turn. There could be pedestrians crossing, a
          traffic hold-up or a car waiting to turn out of the side road,
          in a bad position, making it impossible for you to enter the
          road. If it is not safe to turn you must stop as explained in
          (a) above until it is safe to continue. It is no good realising
          that you cannot enter into the side road when you are over
          half-way across the road thereby blocking the main road
          and endangering oncoming traffic.
          Another reason for looking into the side road as you
          approach is to see exactly where the centre of the road is to
          enable you to stop or, if possible, turn in the correct
          position. I have seen many drivers, not only learners, miss
          the road altogether or mount the pavement because they
          have not looked to see the exact position of the side
          road.
   (*c*)   Look in the mirror before you turn, especially if you have
          had to stop in the centre before turning. There could be a
          motorcycle or even another car trying to pass you on the
          right even though you are signalling correctly.
2.   *Turning left into a side road*   (see Fig. 5)
   (*a*)   Look into the side road as you approach to see if your entry
          to the road is blocked or restricted. Remember that if
          pedestrians are crossing the side road you must give way.
   (*b*)   You should already be aware of any cyclists or motor-
          cyclists and have taken action accordingly but a final check

in the mirror should be made just to make sure there is no danger to others.

3. *Turning into a main road ('T' Junction)*

You must look RIGHT, LEFT and RIGHT AGAIN before you enter the main road. Where there is a STOP sign with double continuous white lines on the road you must stop at the lines. At most 'T' junctions there are give way lines (double broken white lines often with a GIVE WAY sign), where you can continue, without stopping if it is safe to do so.

Where there is a GIVE WAY sign you should start looking right some metres before you reach the junction to give yourself a chance to see if it is safe for you to continue. Having looked to the right and seen that it is clear, you must then look left and if it is still clear, look right again. By that time you should almost be at the double broken white line and if it is still clear you can continue into the main road. If, when you looked in any direction there was any doubt about the safety to proceed, then STOP at the white lines.

If you decide to stop at the junction you must look again in the correct way (RIGHT, LEFT and RIGHT AGAIN) before moving off. Having stopped at the broken white lines you might find that you cannot see to the right and left because of parked vehicles in the main road. If this is the case you should move forward very slowly, controlling the clutch, until you can see if the road is clear. You must then stop, look RIGHT, LEFT and RIGHT AGAIN, and if it is safe proceed carefully into the main road.

The most common and most dangerous faults when turning into a main road are:

(*a*) Not looking RIGHT, LEFT and RIGHT AGAIN when turning LEFT.

Remember that although you might expect other vehicles to be on the lefthand side of the main road when they are coming from your left, this is not always the case. A large vehicle could be overtaking another vehicle, or passing a stationary vehicle and would therefore be almost completely on the righthand side of the road. If you do not look left before emerging, you could drive straight into the front of that large vehicle. There could also be pedestrians crossing the main road to your left.

(*b*) Looking RIGHT, LEFT and RIGHT AGAIN too late so that you are still looking as you enter the main road. If you do this there is nothing that you can do if you see another vehicle coming, except let it hit you!

(*c*) Looking too early. This could mean that you have not seen the road properly and wrongly decide that it is clear when it is not.

(*d*) Not looking at all until you have reached the junction. This is bad driving partly because you may miss an easy opportunity to continue without stopping, thereby wasting time; partly, you would possibly frighten the life out of other motorists when they see you coming up to the end of a road without looking. They could think that you are going to pull straight out into the main road in front of them which could cause an accident if they took evasive action. You may know that you are going to stop but other motorists do not!

Golden rule at junctions

In the first few lessons you will be told to stop at all junctions because until you have familiarised yourself with the routine and the controls of the car it would be foolish to try to continue on at these places. It will not be long, however, before you can decide for yourself whether to stop or continue.

You will also find that your judgement of the speed and distance of other vehicles approaching you will improve with practice. At first you will have to rely on the judgement of your instructor. But remember, the golden rule is:

IF IN DOUBT YOU MUST STOP AT THE JUNCTION

Summary of junction routine   (see Fig. 4)

We will now summarise the routine for approaching junctions.

1.   Look in the mirror early. Then, if safe,
2.   Signal.
3.   Get into the correct position.
4.   Slow car with brake and change down to lower gears.
5.   Look at the junction and be prepared to stop if necessary.

It is only by constant practice that you will be able to gain experience at the many different types of junctions and the situations that can arise at them. The basic routine is the same at all junctions so make sure that you always stick to the correct order.

The procedure at crossroads and junctions with traffic lights will be discussed later in the book. (Crossroads page 89. Traffic Lights page 73.)

Warning signs when approaching bends and junctions
There are usually signs to warn that you are approaching a bend or junction. The warning signs for bends give information about the type of bend, i.e. if the bend is to the left, right, or, in the case of a double bend, which way the bend turns first. Where a bend is considered to be dangerous the word 'SLOW' is often painted on the road surface to warn you to be extra careful. Do not presume, however, that just because there is not a 'SLOW' sign painted in the road, that the approaching bend is not dangerous. The road could have been recently resurfaced and the 'SLOW' sign not repainted yet!

The warning signs for junctions give information as to the type of junction that you are approaching. It could be a 'T' junction, a crossroads, a staggered junction or a 'Y' junction. The sign will also tell you whether a side road is on the left or right and, if it is a staggered junction, which side the first road is situated. There are also markings on the road surface to show which traffic should give way or stop and the centre white line and lane markings give useful information (see page 137).

You should consult the *Highway Code* for further information concerning all the useful traffic signs.

These warning signs for bends and junctions are very helpful, therefore you must look out for them while you are driving and act upon the information that they give you.

Emerging safely at junctions
Correct positioning and observation are the two essential factors to enable you to emerge safely at a junction. You should study the diagrams (see Figs. 6 and 8) carefully and read the advice on page 159.

When emerging you must not cause danger or inconvenience to other road users. This is especially important when you are turning right out of a side road into a main road. You must make certain that the road is clear in both directions before you emerge. You should never move half-way across the road thereby blocking one lane of traffic; always wait in the correct position (i.e. at the double white lines) until it is safe to complete the turn in one movement if you are on a two-way road. The correct procedure for emerging at a dual carriageway is explained on page 132.

Braking

In the section on junctions which you have just read, you will have noticed how important the brake is for slowing the car, and yet in the small amount of driving that you did in the first lesson you hardly used the brake at all. It would be opportune therefore to explain some of the points about braking before the next lesson so that you can quickly overcome some of the problems that all learners experience when slowing down or stopping the car.

Progressive braking
You must apply the brakes progressively when slowing or stopping the car so that the car reduces speed gradually and smoothly. To do this it is necessary to start braking early with gentle pressure on the brake pedal. When you feel the car beginning to slow down you can increase the pressure on the brake pedal slightly so that you will reduce speed at the required rate. As you gain experience your judgement, which is such a vital factor when braking, will improve, enabling you to know just how much to brake for any given situation and allow you to adjust your braking accordingly.

The amount of braking needed can vary greatly depending upon the type of road surface, the gradient of the road, the weight of the vehicle, the weather and how quickly you react to certain situations.

Provided that the brakes are working efficiently, you will find that it is possible to stop the car relatively quickly if needed, but this kind of course necessitates hard braking which can cause a skid and loss of control. When the car is not travelling in a straight line the possibility of losing control is very high, and therefore you must brake before cornering or taking a bend. To brake while you are turning is asking for trouble. (See **Skidding**, page 119.)

Braking when stopping
Many drivers, not only learners, always stop with a jerk. To avoid

this unpleasant movement, which also damages the brakes and suspension of the car, you should ease your foot off the brake pedal just as the car comes to a stop. You must be ready to put pressure on to the brake pedal again to hold the car if you are on an incline until you have applied the hand brake. By easing your foot off the brake pedal at the last moment you allow the car to roll to a stop in the last few inches. The only times that it is not possible to do this are when you stop on a decline and when stopping in an emergency.

Response of the brakes
You have not yet had a chance to get the 'feel' of the brakes on the car that you are driving, but with practice you will discover how the brakes respond to the amount of pressure that you apply to the brake pedal. Later, when you drive other cars, you must be sure that you know how the brakes respond before you need to use them. Do not expect brakes in other cars to respond in the same way as the car you have been used to. As early as possible after you drive off, try the brakes (make sure it is safe to do so) to get the feel of them.

Common faults when braking
1. Not starting to brake early enough, causing late, harsh braking.
2. Lifting the foot off the brake pedal when declutching to change down gear when approaching junctions, causing the car to increase speed if travelling downhill.
3. Braking when taking corners or bends causing possible loss of control.
4. Not easing off the brake at the moment of stopping, causing a jerky stop.
5. Not keeping the brake pedal depressed until the hand brake is applied when stopping on a hill causing the car to roll back.
6. Not taking into account weather conditions and road surface, causing possible loss of control.
7. Not taking into account the gradient of the road and/or the weight of the vehicle causing you to misjudge the amount of braking needed.
8. Not getting the feel of the response of the brakes on the vehicle that you are driving.

Notes for the instructor

Braking is one of the most important skills to be mastered when learning to drive but it is often neglected. Possibly this is because it appears to be so easy just to press a pedal down to make the car stop. Only by practice and learning by his mistakes when braking will the pupil learn how to use the brakes in the proper way.

Do not rush a pupil at junctions

When junctions are practised in Lesson 2 you will find that the instructions to the pupil are started very early, about 90 metres (100 yards) before the junction. At this stage it is advisable to leave as much time as possible but as the pupil gains in skill he will be able to do the MSM manoeuvre in slightly less time.

If the pupil stops at the end of the road but cannot see if it is clear to move off because of an obstruction (e.g. parked van or roadworks) he should move forward slowly into the other road until he can see. You must be careful when he does this because very often a learner will move forward slowly to a position where he can see and then shoot straight out into the road without bothering to stop and look correctly. If you are not ready for this it can take you by surprise and as your vision is probably obscured it can obviously be very dangerous. Always make the pupil stop when he has reached a position where he can see.

You should read the advice on page 159 concerning emerging safely at junctions.

The Second Lesson – Practice

Duration of lesson approximately one hour

Start this lesson in the same road as Lesson 1. For the first few minutes practise the things learned in the first lesson – procedure before starting the engine, moving off on the level, stopping and changing gear. Do not expect the pupil to remember very much. Go through everything with him, and if he has any trouble or appears to have forgotten anything, then spend time explaining it to him. Remember, he is still getting used to the feel of the car and that everything must be dictated to him for the first few lessons.

When this is done, tell him to stop on an incline that is not too steep. You can then explain:

Moving off uphill (gradient)

The only differences between moving off uphill and moving off on level ground is that slightly more acceleration is necessary and if the hand brake is released before the car is being held by the clutch then the car will roll back.

The car is held as before, by bringing up the clutch to the point where the two metal discs (clutch plates) meet. This, remember, is called the 'biting point' or 'point of contact'.

The important thing is to judge when you have brought the clutch up to the 'biting point'. When the clutch reaches the 'biting point' the engine will drop in tone. We call this the 'change of sound'. Once the change of sound is reached you must hold the clutch in that position so that when the hand brake is released, the car will be held by the clutch.

It is vital not to bring the clutch up any higher than the change of sound because the car would try to move before the hand brake is released, and you will stall the engine.

We will now practise it.
1.   *Depress clutch.*
2.   *Select 1st gear.*
3.   *Find correct amount of acceleration. The steeper the hill, the more acceleration will be needed. Remember, once the correct amount of acceleration is found, keep it there.*
4.   *Lift the clutch gently until the change of sound is heard. Then hold the clutch in that position.*

You will have a tendency to lift the clutch too far at first. Once the change of sound has been found, put a little more pressure on the clutch to ensure that you hold it in the correct position. (This counteracts the upward push of the clutch pedal.)

5.   *Release the hand brake.*

If you have lifted the clutch too high, then the hand brake and engine are working against each other, making the hand brake very difficult to release. Always watch for this, because it often causes a lot of problems, especially later when you are trying to do a hill start under pressure (e.g. at traffic lights or busy junctions).

Once the hand brake is released, the car should not move. If the clutch is too high, then the car will move forward. If it is not high enough, then the car will roll back.

You must make sure that the car does not move forward when the hill start is being practised. If the car can be held with the hand brake released then you are sure he has proper control. Luck must play no part in this exercise.

Once the pupil is holding the car on the clutch for a few seconds, get him to depress the clutch very slightly to allow the car to roll back a few feet and then to bring it back up to hold the car still.

The opposite can then be practised, that is, lifting the clutch slightly to let the car move forward a few feet, and then depressing it slightly to hold the car steady again.

If, which is often the case, you lose control of the clutch or accelerator, then practise the start again from the beginning until you can control it properly. I have found this practice essential, because you must get the feel of the clutch as soon as possible.

Without this all else is wasted. Remember that soon you will be venturing out into some traffic, and unless you have had adequate practice on controlling the clutch and feel reasonably confident about controlling it, great difficulties will arise later.

(It is realised that a certain amount of wear is going to be inflicted on the clutch mechanism but holding the clutch at the 'biting point' need only be practised for a few seconds at a time. It will not harm the car for this short period.)

As soon as you have got the feel of the clutch and understood its control, it will not need to be practised again in this manner.

Once you are sure that the pupil is holding the car with the clutch correctly, you can move on.

6. *While holding the clutch at the biting point look in the mirror and over your right shoulder, give a right signal if necessary and if the road is clear . . .*

7. *Lift the clutch slightly to let the car pull away. (Any quick movement of the clutch at this point will cause the car to jump or stall.) Once the car has moved away, gently lift the foot completely off the clutch. Pressure on the accelerator can then be slightly increased.*

You should now continue driving, changing gears at the correct time. Allow that much extra speed when going uphill for changing to 2nd gear, or, preferably, let the car get to the top of the hill before changing at this stage – depending on the length of the hill.

As soon as possible stop the pupil again on a hill to practise the hill start. This must be repeated several times. It is not necessary to make the pupil roll the car backwards and forwards any more but make sure that he holds the car still on the clutch for one second before actually moving off. This must be done on all hill starts otherwise you cannot tell whether he is actually controlling the clutch or not.

Continue practising the hill start at intervals throughout the next few lessons.

At the earliest opportunity you should tell the pupil to stop the car on a down gradient to enable you to teach him how to move away down a hill. Although this is basically less difficult than moving away elsewhere it can cause a problem if the pupil does not practise one or two down hill starts before driving on the more difficult roads.

Depending on the layout of the particular roads that you are on you can either teach moving off down a hill before you teach the junctions, or if it is more convenient you can practise one or two junctions before teaching the downhill start.

When the opportunity arises, tell the pupil to stop on a decline. You can then explain:

Moving off downhill

It is impossible to hold the car with the clutch when moving off downhill, therefore, you must apply the foot brake before the hand brake is released, otherwise the car will move forward before you are ready.

We will now practise it.
1. *Depress clutch and select 1st gear.*
2. *Depress brake.*
3. *Release hand brake making sure that you are holding the car stationary with the foot brake.*
4. *Look in the mirror and over your right shoulder, if the road is clear . . .*
5. *Lift your foot off the brake.*
6. *Lift clutch smoothly and at the same time accelerate slightly.*

You will find that the clutch can be lifted more quickly than when moving off on the level because the car is already moving, but be careful not to snatch your foot off the clutch because a jumpy start will result.

It is the moving of the right foot from the brake pedal to the accelerator that can cause the most problems. Having practised it a few times, however, you will become quite fluent with the technique.

Left turns

The next stage is to practise left turns. Remember that all corners must be approached in 2nd (or 1st) gear so give the pupil plenty of time to change down the gears. It does not matter at first if he changes slightly too early into the low gears because these gear changes can be difficult for him at this stage. It is important that the approach to the first few turnings are reasonably flat because any steep gradient could make the junction extremely difficult.

There are two types of left turns: (*a*) turning left into a side road, and (*b*) turning left into a main road, i.e. T-junction.

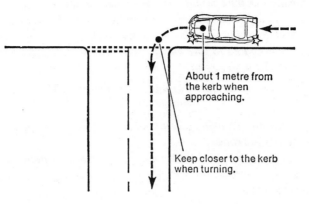

About 1 metre from
the kerb when
approaching.

Keep closer to the kerb
when turning.

Fig. 5 Position when turning left into a side road.

A. Turning left into a side road (off a main road)   (See Fig. 5)
We will take this first for convenience, but in practice it does not
matter which one you take first.

When you are a good distance from the road, about 90 metres (100
yards) and in 3rd or 4th gear, give him the instruction:

I want you to turn left at the next road.
1.   Check mirror (must be done very early).

Remind the pupil that he should be looking especially for bicycles and
motorcycles that could come up on the left.

2.   Signal intention to turn left (if safe to do so).
3.   Slow down slightly with brake (if necessary) and change to 2nd
*   gear.*

2nd gear should be engaged about 20 metres (21 yards) before the
corner. You must talk him through the gear change.

4.   Release clutch gently.

Always watch for this because if he develops a habit of keeping the
clutch down at this stage it will be very difficult to break later.

5.   Keep about 1 metre (3–4 feet) away from the kerb as you
*   approach the corner. This is very important because if the car is*

too close to the kerb it will be impossible to keep in the correct position when turning the corner. Either the back wheels will hit the kerb or the car will turn the corner too far from the kerb.

6.   *When the front of the car reaches the corner of the road, turn the wheel to the left (no crossing of hands!).*

   Be prepared to give way to pedestrians who could be already crossing the side road.

Be ready to help him turn the wheel because he will have difficulty in gauging the amount of steering needed.

Look in the direction that you intend the car to go, and when the car is straight with the road . . .

7.   *Straighten the wheel (again without crossing the hands).*

   Never increase the speed of the car until the wheel has been straightened.

Your left foot should be over the clutch when approaching and turning the corner but must not be depressing it.

   (No acceleration must be used while beginning to turn the corner unless there is a slight uphill gradient. The car should continue round the corner at an idling speed with just enough acceleration to keep it moving at the same speed in 2nd gear until the wheel is straightened. The car must be at its slowest while beginning to turn the corner.)

   The main things to watch out for are that you do not swing out just before turning the corner and that the car does not increase speed just before straightening up. Remember that it is difficult to gauge how much you have turned the wheel so you may not always straighten up enough at first.

B.   Turning left into a main road from a side road. ('T' junction)
(See Fig. 6)

Although it is not always necessary to stop at a 'T' junction, it is advisable in the early stages to do so. This will enable you to master the correct procedure for moving away. Once this has been prac- tised a few times, then the instructor can use his discretion as to which ones you should stop at and which you can continue on. (It is best to agree this at the earliest stage otherwise you may think that you have to stop at every junction.) Broken double white lines do

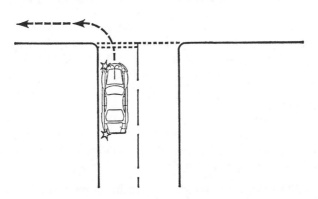

Fig. 6   Position when turning left into a main road.

not mean stop; they are GIVE WAY lines. It is only the continuous double white lines that mean stop. I will be elaborating on this in later lessons (page 142). When you are about 90 metres (100 yards) or so from the junction (in 3rd gear), give him the instruction:

I want you to turn left at the end of the road.
1. *Check mirror.*
2. *Signal intention to turn left (if safe to do so).*
3. *Slow down slightly with brake (if necessary) and change to 2nd gear.*

2nd gear should be engaged about 20 metres (21 yards) before the corner. (You must talk him through the gear change.)

4. *Release the clutch.*

This could cause a problem at first. If you have been slow getting into 2nd gear, you will not have time to lift the clutch before you have to put it down again for stopping at the end of the road. It is important, however, that you should make the effort at least to start lifting the clutch and not just keep your foot down until you stop. If the clutch is not lifted it could cause bigger problems later, especially if you change to 2nd gear too early and then just coast to the end of the road with your foot depressing the clutch.

5.   *Stop at the end of the road, not too close to the kerb, and slightly turning the wheel to the left as you stop. The front wheels should then be turned slightly in the direction that you want to go.*

You must approach the left turn some distance from the kerb, just under a metre (2½ feet or so), only turning the wheel slightly at the very last moment before stopping. If the corner is approached too closely, then either the back wheels will hit the kerb or the corner will have to be taken too wide to avoid this happening. This applies to all left turns.

Make sure that you have not stopped too far back so as not to be able to see down the road properly, nor too far forward so that the front of the car is endangering traffic in the other road.

It is difficult to judge this at first but try to drive right up to the end of the road before stopping.

6.   *Only apply the hand brake if you are on an incline or if you are at a stop sign. It is unnecessary for the hand brake to be used otherwise, unless the stop is likely to be of longer duration than just a few seconds.*
7.   *Select 1st gear.*

Make sure you keep your foot firmly down on the clutch while waiting at the junction.

8.   *Accelerate slightly (listen for the purring sound).*
9.   *LOOK RIGHT, LEFT AND RIGHT AGAIN.*

You must get in the habit of looking correctly right, left and right again from the beginning. So many pupils just look right and left before emerging. This is dangerous and almost a certain failure in the driving test.

10. *If the road is clear, move away by lifting the clutch just to the 'biting point' so that you can control the car with the clutch while you steer round the corner. In other words, as the car starts to move, keep your foot in that position on the clutch while you turn the wheel (without crossing hands) round the corner, and keep your foot controlling the clutch until you have straightened the wheel. Once you have straightened the wheel and the car is*

going in the direction required, then, and only then, can the rest
of the clutch be gently released.

It is best for the pupil to slightly over-exaggerate this at first, because
one of the most common faults is to snatch the clutch off suddenly
before the wheel has been straightened. This can have disastrous
results and you must be ready for it.

Continue the pupil round the block taking as many left turns as
possible. Never rush him at the junctions, let him do it in his own time.

When the left turns have been practised for some minutes you can
then go on to right turns. The procedure will be about the same, but
there are a couple of extra hazards when turning right, concerning
positioning and other traffic which must be emphasised.

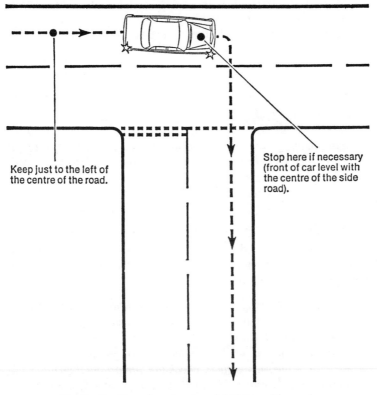

Fig. 7   Position when turning right into a side road.

Right turns

There are two types of right turns: (*a*) turning into a side road on the
right and (*b*) turning at the end of a road, i.e. road junction.

A.   Turning right into a side road (from a main road) (See Fig. 7)
Again we will take (*a*) first, but in practice it does not matter which
you take. When you are at least 90 metres (100 yards) from the road
and in 3rd or 4th gear, give him the instruction:

I want you to turn right at the next road.
1.   *Check mirror (must be done early).*
2.   *Signal intention to turn right (if safe to do so).*
3.   *Move into correct position. This is just to the left of the centre of
     the road (crown of the road).*
4.   *Slow down slightly on brake (if necessary) and change into 2nd
     gear.*

2nd gear should be engaged about 20 metres (21 yards) before the
corner.

5.   *Release the clutch gently.*
6a. *If there is no oncoming traffic and it is safe to turn the corner
     without stopping, when you get level with the centre of the road
     into which you are intending to go: turn the wheel to the right and
     when the car is straight and in the direction you want it to go,
     straighten the wheel.*
     *Make sure you keep the same very slow speed while turning the
     corner.*

No acceleration should be necessary but watch you do not slow
down too much. Be ready to accelerate slightly otherwise you could
stall in the middle of the turn.

6b. *If there is oncoming traffic and it is not safe to turn, you must stop
     with the front of the car level with the centre of the road into
     which you are turning.*
7.   *Select 1st gear and keep the right indicator going.*
8.   *Wait until the road is clear, check the mirror and then move off,
     controlling the clutch and turning the wheel at the same time. Do
     not lift your foot right off the clutch until you have straightened*

> *the wheel unless it is a very wide turning. Certainly do not increase your speed until you have completed the turn.*

Make sure that you turn the wheel immediately the car starts to move. Sometimes, in worrying about the control of the clutch, you may forget to turn the wheel.

If you have to stop before turning you must check the mirror before moving off from the centre of the road.

It is also important that the instructor looks behind because motorists often try to overtake on the right of a learner, even though he is signalling, especially if he is slow in moving away.

Your positioning is the main thing to look for. It is essential that you get into the habit of correct positioning from the start.

When approaching the right turn some pupils are very hesitant about moving across into the correct position, even after having checked their mirror and given the signal for turning right. Move across as early as possible after you have made sure it is safe, otherwise when you get into busier roads you will find it very difficult.

When you are approaching this type of right turn, you should glance at the road to check where the centre of the road is so that you can stop or turn in the correct position, i.e. level with the centre of the side road. Very often a learner can miss the road altogether by not glancing at the side road. This most commonly occurs when a vehicle is approaching in the opposite direction and the learner is hoping that it will pass just in time for him to continue round the corner without stopping. If there is the slightest doubt that the road will not be clear by the time you get level with the centre of the road you must stop. In a situation like this it is better for the inexperienced learner to stop unnecessarily than either to miss the turning altogether by going too far, or worse still, to cause an accident by turning before the other car has passed.

B. Turning right into a main road from a side road. ('T' junction)
(See Fig. 8)

Similar to turning left but again positioning is all important. When at least 90 metres (100 yards) from the junction, give him the instruction:

I want you to turn right at the end of the road.
1. *Check the mirror (must be done early).*

2.   *Signal intention to turn right (if safe to do so).*
3.   *Move into correct position (just to the left of the centre of road).*
4.   *Slow down slightly with brake (if necessary) and change into 2nd gear.*
5.   *Release clutch but be ready to depress clutch again before stopping.*
6.   *Stop at the end of the road to the left of the centre. You must allow enough room for cars to turn into the side road.*

It is not always sufficient to be just to the left of the centre of the road. If it is a very narrow road then you must be well over to the left to allow other vehicles to enter the road.

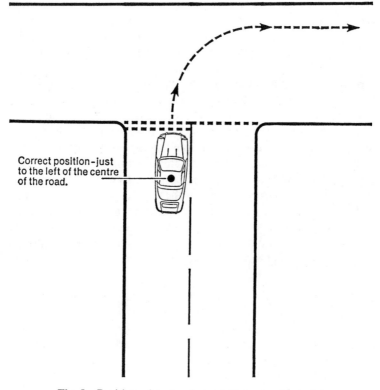

Correct position–just to the left of the centre of the road.

Fig. 8   Position when turning right into a main road.

7. *Apply hand brake only if necessary.*
8. *Select 1st gear.*
9. *LOOK RIGHT, LEFT AND RIGHT AGAIN.*
10. *Move off, controlling the clutch and turning the wheel at the same time.*
11. *Straighten the wheel when the car is straight with the road, keeping control with the clutch.*
12. *Release the clutch gently.*

A common fault on moving off here is that you do not begin to turn the wheel immediately the car moves, but wait until you pass the centre of the road and then turn. This is either because you are concentrating on the clutch so much that you forget about turning the wheel (as explained earlier) or you think that you must go past the centre of the road that you are going into before starting to turn the wheel.

When turning right out of a road always beware of the vehicle that is turning into the road. If the vehicle is coming from your left and is turning right into your road, make sure that you wait until the vehicle has completed his turn. It is very easy to pull out too early and catch the tail of the other vehicle. Remember that the other car may slow down or even stop before he enters the road.

If a vehicle is coming from your right and signalling its intention to turn left into your road, do not presume that he will turn. The driver could be signalling because he is stopping, turning left at another road, or even forgot that his indicator was on. Many accidents have occurred because signalling has been misinterpreted in this way.

Keep practising these left and right turns on the quiet roads until the pupil becomes reasonably happy with them.

General points about left and right turns

It must be remembered at this stage that 4th gear may not have been used and therefore all of these turnings may have only necessitated a change from 3rd gear into 2nd. When it is possible for you to use 4th gear you should do so. When approaching junctions you can change directly from 4th gear into 2nd gear. It is not necessary to engage 3rd gear as you approach the junction at all in these circumstances. You just move the gear lever directly from 4th to 2nd gear. You should be the same distance from the junction when you engage 2nd gear, whether you are changing from 4th or 3rd gear (about 20 metres). However, the fact that you are approaching in 4th gear will mean that when you take your foot from the accelerator, the car will not slow down as much as it would if you were in 3rd gear. It is therefore essential that you use the footbrake correctly to slow the car before and whilst you engage 2nd gear. Remember that you should be travelling about 10 miles per hour when you select 2nd gear. This is very important when approaching a junction on a decline, when the brake should be applied immediately after you have looked in the mirror to check that it is safe to do so. The earlier the braking, the less pressure will be needed and much smoother braking will result.

The pupil will have trouble in judging the amount of braking necessary and you will have to help him verbally by just saying 'Ease off the brake' or alternatively, 'Just a little more brake'. Make sure that you say this calmly otherwise you may panic him and cause a sudden stab on the brake.

You must give him adequate warning when you wish him to turn a corner. Always make sure that he knows exactly which road you want him to take. Never cause the pupil to rush into anything.

Impress on the pupil the correct order: MIRROR – SIGNAL – MANOEUVRE.

Most common faults

1. Pupil lifts off the brake when depressing the clutch to change gear. This can cause the car to increase speed especially if descending a hill.
2. Not lifting the clutch right up before turning into a side road. This would mean that the engine was not controlling the car and could cause the car to increase speed just at the wrong moment.

Both these points must be watched for very carefully. Bad habits must not be allowed to get a hold!

Downhill junctions

When waiting to move off at a junction that is on a downward gradient, the hand brake is not necessary. The car can be held safely on the foot brake. When the road is clear you can then just lift your foot off the foot brake and the car will move. You can then bring up the clutch and accelerate at the same time.

It is important to practise this type of junction because, although it is in some ways easier than moving off on the flat, it can cause confusion in the mind of the learner. He will probably forget to turn the wheel when the car moves, waiting until he has brought up the clutch. Watch for this! Make sure that he turns the wheel as soon as the car begins to move into the road. Once again it is a case of his getting confident of his control of the car.

The Third Lesson – Preparation

Having now completed the first two lessons you should be getting the 'feel' of how the car responds to the controls and be more familiar with the position of the controls. As you gain in practice you will find that this 'feeling' for the response of the controls will improve until eventually the car will be so much a part of you when you are driving that it will feel like an extension of yourself; eventually you will act with the correct response as you see situations occur ahead of you.

You have, so far, kept to the minor roads which have needed very limited use of the gears but when you drive for further distances on the larger roads in the next few lessons you will find that the use of the gears will increase. This is a good time to give you some more information about why and when you change gear and how to change gear smoothly.

Gears

Reason for having different gears

There are only two essential gears in a motor vehicle, one forward and one reverse. These two gears would enable the vehicle to move forwards or backwards and, in fact, most vehicles do have only one reverse gear. Why then, have more than one forward gear?

If you think of the engine as yourself, actually pushing the vehicle, you can imagine how difficult it would be for you to move the vehicle from a stationary position. You would have to find a very strong person to help you. Let us imagine then, that you enlist the help of a heavy weight-lifter to help. He would no doubt move the car away successfully but, as a weight-lifter is not exactly built for speed, you would find that your progress would be very slow. Once the weight-lifter had managed to move the vehicle from a stationary position, you would then have to find somebody built for slightly more speed than power, to continue pushing the vehicle to enable you to increase the speed. If you then keep changing each person for another who could run faster you would gradually increase the speed of the car until you had an Olympic sprinter pushing the car at the maximum speed.

If you had to slow the car down for any reason the Olympic sprinter would find it impossible, because of his lack of power, to continue pushing the car at the lower speed. You would have to call on one of the others, possibly even the weight-lifter, if you had slowed down to almost stationary, to push the car and gradually build up speed again.

The stronger man could help you to actually slow down because if, as well as using the brake yourself, one of the powerful men helped to pull you back, the car would decrease speed more efficiently. The Olympic sprinter would not have the power to help slow the speed of the car.

These men, then, are the gears. They help the engine to move the car more easily. The Olympic runner is the 4th gear (top gear). This is the gear that enables the car to travel at the maximum speed using the least possible amount of power. This is the gear that you normally drive in once you have reached a speed of about 25 mph.

The other helpers are the other gears. You can have as many gears as are needed. On very large vehicles there can be as many as fifteen different gears but most cars have either three, four or five. Each successively lower gear gives more power but with correspondingly less speed until you come to the 'heavy weight-lifter' which is 1st gear. The lower the road speed of the vehicle, the lower the gear that needs to be selected to keep full control of the vehicle.

When to change gear

There is no exact speed at which you should change gear. It is advisable always to move off from a stationary position in 1st gear. The speed at which you change into the other gears will depend on several factors including the type and size of car, the power of the engine, the number of passengers in the car and whether you are travelling uphill, downhill or on the level.

The approximate speeds at which you should change gear on the level are as follows:

Moving off	1st gear
5 mph	2nd gear
15 mph	3rd gear
25 mph	4th gear

To look at the speedometer while you are driving is not advisable because you would have to take your eyes off the road, therefore, you have to judge the speed of the car and listen to the sound of the engine. As the car increases speed the sound of the engine will increase and you will get to know, with more experience, the particular sound at which you should change gear. At this stage of learning you have to rely on your instructor to tell you when to change up or down the gears but if you make an effort to listen to the sound of the engine it will not be long before you are changing gear at the same time as he is telling you to. You will probably be able to change up to higher gears at the correct time at an earlier stage of learning than you will be to change down, because it is more difficult to judge when to change down. You have to rely much more on your judgement of the relative speed of the car when you change down gears because there is no change of engine sound. You will find, however, that the car labours (shudders) slightly if you are in a gear that is too high for the speed of the car and this is a sign to tell you to change down to a lower gear.

As stated earlier, when we were discussing junctions, it is usual to change down to 2nd gear before turning a sharp corner. When approaching a hazard you should slow down and therefore 3rd gear or even 2nd gear is usually necessary.

Technique of changing gears

Changing up
In Lessons 1 and 2 you were shown, and you practised, the basic technique for changing to higher gears. No doubt you have found it difficult to accomplish the gear changes smoothly. Do not worry too much about this because with more practice you will find that

your co-ordination will improve, making the gear changes less jumpy.

To be able to change to a higher gear smoothly it is important that your right foot is lifted off the accelerator as you put down the clutch before you change the gear and that you accelerate as you bring up the clutch after changing the gear. This timing is very precise and can only improve gradually with practice.

Provided that you do not take your foot off the clutch with a jerky movement, that the car is travelling at the correct speed and that you obey the principles in the above paragraph, you will change gear smoothly.

Changing down

In the earlier lessons you have had very limited practice at changing down to a lower gear because of the relatively slow speed at which you have been driving. You probably found it slightly more difficult than changing to a higher gear. One reason for this is that very often you are approaching a hazard, or about to turn a corner when you have to change down to a lower gear and this puts you under more pressure than when you are changing up gears. Try not to rush the actual gear change, especially when coming down to 2nd gear from 3rd or 4th gear. It is quite a difficult movement and the chances are that if you try to do it too quickly, you will miss the correct gear. This is where the importance of correct braking before changing down to 2nd gear can be seen because if you have not slowed the car down sufficiently you will find it difficult to change into 2nd gear without rushing. You will also find that if you select the wrong gear by mistake you will have time to change back into the correct gear if you have used the brake sufficiently to slow the car.

Matching road speed with engine speed

To change down gears smoothly it is vital to match the road speed of the car with the speed (or revolutions) of the engine, or vice versa. It is possible to do this either by using the brake to slow the car down to the correct speed or by keeping the engine revs going by keeping your foot gently on the accelerator pedal while you change down to a lower gear. So far in the lessons you have been using the former method (i.e. slowing down with the brake before changing down gears), and it is advisable to continue using this method whenever you are approaching junctions, especially when changing down to 2nd gear. The reason that this method is advised is that when you are approaching a junction it is confusing, until you have gained much more experience, to keep your foot on the accelerator while at the same time trying to slow the car down.

There are occasions, however, when it may be necessary for you to use the latter method. For instance, when you change down from 4th gear to 3rd while travelling at about 30 mph when approaching a bend or other hazard, or when you are about to overtake a moving vehicle. Braking would not be needed in these circumstances so if you keep your foot gently on the accelerator as you change into 3rd gear you will find that there will be a smooth transition from 4th gear to 3rd gear.

When you change down to 1st gear while the car is moving at a very slow speed, it is again advisable to accelerate slightly to ensure a smooth gear change. The reason for this is that you would already have slowed the car with the brake to almost a stop before you used 1st gear and it would therefore be more important to keep the car moving slowly than to use the brake, which would stop the car. By accelerating slightly as you change down to 1st gear, the engine revs match road speed which should eliminate any difficulty in engaging this gear. If you are driving an older car without synchromesh on 1st gear then it is essential that you 'double-declutch' when changing down.

Double-declutching

Most cars have what is known as synchromesh on all the gears. However, some do not have synchromesh on first gear and on many older cars the synchromesh does not work very well on the lower gears. Synchromesh matches the speed of the gear wheels when you change gear so that they do not smash together causing a dreadful scraping noise, therefore, if you have synchromesh on your gears it enables you to change down gear in the way we have already described.

Double-declutching is the technique of changing down gear to be used if you are changing into a lower gear without synchromesh. The procedure is as follows:

1. Clutch pedal down, at the same time release accelerator pedal.
2. Move gear lever into neutral and keep it there.
3. Clutch pedal up, at the same time push on and off accelerator pedal.
4. Clutch pedal down, change to lower gear.
5. Clutch pedal up, at the same time depress the accelerator.

The faster the car is travelling the harder you have to put your foot down on the accelerator when you have put the gear lever into neutral. The reason for this is that you have to get the speed of the engine up to the road speed of the car to match the gear wheels. A quick on and off movement with the accelerator is the best technique in these circumstances.

It is not an easy technique to master so it will mean quite a lot of practice before the co-ordination is perfected. Find a nice quiet road to practise this if it is necessary.

Sequence of traffic lights

It is surprising that many experienced drivers do not know the sequence of traffic lights, or exactly what each coloured light means. It is important to learn the sequence of traffic lights and their meaning early in your driving lessons so that by the time you take the driving test you are familiar with them. Not only does the examiner often ask a question about them, but he can also see by the way you approach and act at traffic lights if you are sure of the sequence and fully understand their meaning.

The sequence and meaning of traffic lights from RED is as follows:

RED means	STOP	(wait behind the white stop line)
RED AND AMBER TOGETHER means	STOP	(Do not cross white stop line until GREEN light)
GREEN means	GO	(If the way ahead is clear and it is safe to do so)
AMBER means	STOP	(at the white stop line unless you have already

passed the white stop line
when the amber light
appears or are so close to
the line that to pull up
might cause an accident)

You can see from the above information that all of the colours mean STOP except for GREEN. Even when it is green you can only go if it is safe to do so. You must be especially careful to look out for pedestrians not only when you turn left or right (when you must give way to them if they are crossing the road) but also when you go straight on at the lights. Remember, if many experienced drivers do not know the meaning of the lights, then you cannot expect many pedestrians to know the meaning of them either.

Filter lights

When a green arrow shows on a set of traffic lights it means you go in the direction of the arrow, if it is safe to do so, irrespective of any other light which is showing at the same time.

Lights at pelican crossings

The procedure and sequence is exactly the same as above except that instead of the red and amber light before the green, there is a flashing amber light. This means that you can move off only if there is no pedestrian still using the pelican crossing.

Notes for the instructor

Matching road speed with engine speed (or vice versa) causes problems for instructors and learners. As I stated in the 'Notes to the pupil', it is advisable normally to make the pupil slow the car on the brake to bring the speed of the car down to match the revs of the engine when approaching junctions. Many instruction books, however, advise that the pupil should always accelerate while changing down gears to ensure a smooth change.

In practice I have found that the pupil must brake progressively when approaching a junction so that the vehicle is travelling at below 10 mph when he begins to change down to 2nd gear some 20 metres (21 yards) before the junction. To do this he must keep his foot constantly on the brake while he changes down the gears, unless he is approaching the junction up a hill. To teach him to accelerate while he changes gear could make it very confusing for the pupil and can cause him to panic.

As stated earlier there are times when it is advisable for the pupil to keep his foot slightly on the accelerator and when possible this should be practised, but not when coming down to 2nd gear when approaching junctions.

Changing down more than one gear at a time

This point concerns changing down more than one gear at a time (e.g. 4th gear to 2nd gear). This should be encouraged but in the early lessons it is difficult for the pupil to accomplish the change properly. He will either change far too early, or be travelling too fast for 2nd gear. It will be worth practising this gear change with him paying particular attention to the use of the footbrake.

Changing into first gear while moving
Try to familiarise the pupil with changing into first gear when he is travelling at a very slow speed, especially when approaching 'T' junctions. This will enable him to continue when he has the opportunity, without stopping. Make sure that he still looks properly RIGHT, LEFT AND RIGHT AGAIN before he emerges. To be able to shift into 1st gear easily will also assist him later when he is driving slowly in heavy traffic.

Three-gear cars

Matching road speed with engine speed is even more important in the three-gear car, therefore more practice is essential. Changing down to 1st gear is also more frequent, so you must get the pupil familiar with this. In many three-geared cars it is necessary to 'double-declutch' when changing on 1st gear and the explanation on p. 62 will help to explain this to the pupil.

Traffic lights

During the next lesson you will be driving through traffic lights for the first time. Information on the sequences and meaning of the different colours are on p. 63 and you should read this before the next lesson. Your instructor can help by testing your knowledge on this after you have had a chance of studying it.

There also follows some advice to you on keeping to the left of the road. Incorrect positioning in normal driving is a very common fault with learners and many fail a driving test because of this. Therefore from the earliest stage of learning you should be reminded of the importance of correct positioning.

Keeping to the left in normal driving

When it is possible you should keep to the left of the road at all times. This does not mean just to the left of the centre of the road, but to the left of your side of the road. Endeavour to keep about one metre (3–4 feet) from the kerb when driving normally and make sure you keep well over to the left when you are going straight ahead at traffic lights, crossroads and roundabouts unless the road markings dictate otherwise or there is an obstruction on the left such as parked vehicles or roadworks.

If you are turning right you should normally position the car on the crown of the road, that is just to the left of the centre. Never drive on the wrong side of the road unless an obstruction makes it impossible to do otherwise.

When passing a line of parked cars, there is no need to keep weaving in and out. This would only confuse other road users. It all depends on the size of the gap between the cars, so use your common sense to determine whether it is worth moving back over to the left before pulling out again.

The Third Lesson – Practice

Duration of lesson one hour

Planning your route

It is a good idea to plan out a route before starting this lesson. When deciding on a route, try to make the transition from the small quiet roads to the more difficult roads gradual. In other words, try to avoid taking the pupil from the ground that he knows and where he has developed confidence to somewhere that suddenly seems strange and shatters that confidence. A very difficult right turn into a main road, a tricky uphill turn into a busy, fast road, or a difficult round-about, would not help the pupil at all at this stage.

Begin the lesson from the same place as you started in the other lessons and build your route from there. Towards the end of the lesson you can bring in some more difficult roads, but always let it depend on the progress of the pupil. Let your planned route be flexible. Try to have some alternatives to your route especially in your homeward journey just in case the progress on the lesson is not as good as you anticipated.

Do not take the pupil too far out on a route otherwise by the time you return you will both be getting tired which could cause aggravation. No lesson should be too long at this stage. One hour is quite long enough.

When planning your route for this and the next few lessons, remember that side roads should be used more than main roads. Include plenty of right and left turns, and try to avoid obvious traffic black spots. Of course, if your lessons are on Sundays, the traffic problem should not be too bad anyway.

For this lesson, try to include in your route a couple of sets of traffic lights, a roundabout and a pedestrian crossing.

Make sure that the pupil does everything correctly and in the right order.

Give good clear directions and always remind the pupil to look in the mirror often, but especially before signalling, slowing down or changing direction. It is up to you, as the instructor, to talk the pupil through everything at this stage.

Do not be led into a false sense of security when you find that the pupil appears to be advancing well. Remember he is still very inexperienced, and as soon as something goes wrong, it is up to you to take control of the situation.

Points to remember and some more tips

1. Never take your eyes off the road for more than a second.
2. Try to anticipate when the pupil is going to get into difficulties.
3. Always be ready to lay a steadying hand on the steering wheel, especially when the pupil is changing gear.
4. Never rush the pupil. There will be times when you know that you are holding people up behind you, but try not to let the pupil be put off by it. If you remain calm and cool, then so will he. Just talk him through the correct procedure. He will soon begin to do things a little more quickly. (Mind you, don't let him dawdle along the road when he could quite easily increase his speed safely. Sometimes pupils get into a little world of their own drifting along the road for about half a mile in 2nd gear, at about 15 miles per hour.) Be sure that he makes progress where possible.
5. Do not be surprised if the pupil has difficulty in distinguishing between left and right. At this stage it is very common for pupils to:

    (A) signal left when they are intending to turn right.
    (B) forget which way they have been told to turn.
    (C) suddenly turn in the opposite direction.

    Each mistake needs a different reaction, as follows:

A.   Signalling in wrong direction

This is very common and is usually caused by the pupil being confused about which way the indicator works for signalling left or right. Although you have already explained this to the pupil, it is sometimes difficult for him to remember it when he needs to use it.

The important thing is that you notice the mistake so that no confusion is caused to following traffic. In fact, it is a good idea at this stage to say, after telling the pupil to look in his mirror and signal left, 'that is up'. It helps to impress it upon his mind. When you have a chance, you can go back over the instruction that the indicator goes the same way as the steering wheel. It may not cure him straight away but it will help.

Some pupils just have difficulty telling their left from their right. Only perseverance can help this. It is really up to him to sort it out. He will, but it will take time.

B. Forgetting which way to turn

This often happens when the pupil has reached the junction. It has been some time since the direction was given, and although he is signalling in the correct direction, his mind suddenly goes blank. This is no great problem as long as the instructor is ready for it.

Keep your eye on the wheel as he begins to turn and if you have the slightest doubt of which way he is going, immediately remind him of the direction intended.

I have found that the pupil is often confused when approaching the end of a narrow road to turn right. The order to turn right has been given early and as the pupil gets near to the end of the road he is too far to the right of the road, so you advise him to 'keep to the left to allow other vehicles to turn into the road'. Subconsciously the word 'left' sticks in his mind so that when he moves away at the end of the road he turns left instead of right. This is worth remembering.

C. Suddenly turns in the wrong direction

This is the least common mistake but by far the most dangerous – the driving instructor's nightmare!

The pupil has been told to turn left at the road some 90 metres (100 yards) away. He looks in the mirror, signals left and suddenly turns right into another road, often attempting to turn in 3rd or 4th gear at about 25 miles per hour.

The consequences of this obviously can be disastrous. The only possible reason for doing this, apart from suicide, is that he mistook your directions to turn left for right, and suddenly seeing the road on the right, immediately turns into it.

All that can be advised is to watch out for it. Watch for sudden tenseness, especially with the hands on the wheel. Also look out for turnings on the opposite side of the road which could be potential dangers to absent-minded pupils.

It is important for an instructor to be ready for all such emergencies. Be sure that you can grab the steering wheel easily and quickly. (Remember always go for the lower part of the wheel, under the arms of the pupil, because this is the shortest distance for your hand to travel, and you won't get tangled up with the pupil's own hands.)

Just one other point while we are on this subject. If you have told the pupil to turn left at a busy junction which is controlled by traffic lights, and he goes straight on, it is better to let him continue rather than forcing him to suddenly turn left. It could be safer even if he is signalling left. Always take the easiest and safest way out for the circumstances.

Begin the lesson in the same road as lessons 1 and 2. Go through and practise the things learned in the first two lessons, i.e. procedure before starting engine, moving off on the level, stopping, changing gear, moving off on a hill, turning left and turning right. Use the same roads for a few minutes and then gradually move away from this area into your planned route.

At the earliest opportunity tell the pupil to stop a couple of metres (yards) behind a parked car. He should stop in a position where he can just move away safely. This will enable you to teach him one of the manoeuvres in the test.

Moving off at an angle

Once you have stopped and you have satisfied yourself that you have enough room to move away in forward gear (at first leave a little extra space behind the parked car until you are confident with the manoeuvre), your instructor will then give you the following instruction:

Now I want you to move away from this position. The idea of this manoeuvre is to show that you can pull away safely from behind an obstruction.

The important thing, as with most manoeuvres, is to control the clutch properly. You must keep control of the clutch until you have steered round the car and are safely travelling straight with the road.

The following procedure presumes that you are moving away on the flat or on an incline. If you are on a downhill slope you will have to use the appropriate procedure as on page 46.

1. Depress clutch.
2. Select 1st gear.
3. Find the correct amount of acceleration.
4. Lift the clutch slowly until you find the biting point (listen for the change of sound).
5. Check mirror and look over right shoulder.
6. Signal right. (A signal is necessary here because while you are controlling the car and manoeuvring around the parked vehicle, some seconds will elapse. In this time another vehicle

could approach you, and your signal will warn him of your intentions.)

7. Release hand brake then replace hands on wheel.
8. Start lifting the clutch slowly until you feel the car beginning to pull away. If it is safe to move (and this means you must check in front of you), give another look round for a last check.
9. As the car begins to move, hold the clutch in that position and turn the steering wheel quickly to the right.

   You must clear the parked car by at least ½ metre (2 feet).
10. Keep controlling the car with the clutch until you have cleared the parked car and straightened the wheel.

Some pupils have a tendency to 'freeze' as the car moves forward and forget to turn the wheel. Watch for this and make sure that you turn the wheel quickly. Be ready to stop the car if you feel it is getting too close to the parked vehicle. You can always start again.

The straightening up often causes the biggest problem. Do not let go of the clutch too early, you may not realise how much you have to turn the wheel back again. Keep controlling the clutch while you are straightening up the car.

Don't forget your observation
Remember that observation is of prime importance, not only for vehicles coming up from behind, but also those approaching from opposite direction. Your car may move a long way out on the wrong side of the road, especially if the vehicle you are moving out from is large. You are therefore a danger to oncoming traffic.

This manoeuvre should be practised occasionally from now onwards. It is good for giving you confidence in clutch control and for making you aware of the importance of observation.

If this manoeuvre was not very successful the first time, then try it again later in the lesson. As with all manoeuvres, it is not a good idea to repeat it too many times without a break. Better to leave it for a while, or even until the next lesson, when it will probably be more successful.

Continue on your route. The pupil will now begin to come across some of the hazards on the road. Talk him through everything, including all gear changes. It is important that he gets used to changing gear at the correct time, so it is up to you to tell him when to change. It will be quite a while before he is changing the gear as you are telling him, and that is the time for you to stop talking him through the gear changes. This could take quite a few lessons. When that stage is reached, you can just comment if you consider a gear change to be incorrect.

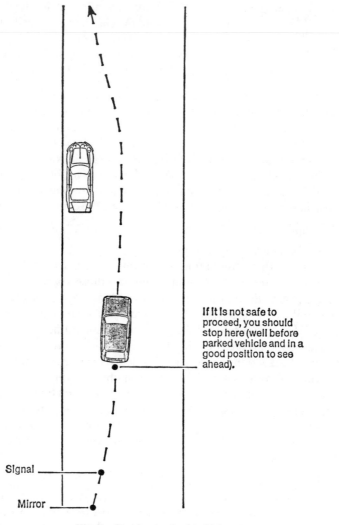

If it is not safe to proceed, you should stop here (well before parked vehicle and in a good position to see ahead).

Signal

Mirror

Fig. 9 Passing parked vehicles.

Passing parked vehicles (See Fig. 9)

Make sure that you check your mirror before pulling out to pass any obstruction such as parked cars, roadworks, etc. Remember that it is only necessary to signal in these circumstances if there is anyone following. There is no reason to signal that you are pulling out from an obstruction if there is nobody behind you unless you are moving off from a stationary position in which case a signal might be helpful to somebody in front.

When approaching a parked car make sure that you check the mirror as soon as possible. You can then decide if a signal is necessary. If there is any doubt then signal straight away. Remember, the earlier you warn other traffic of your intention the better. After looking in your mirror and signalling, if necessary, pull out from the obstruction as early as possible. It is no good waiting until you are almost on top of the vehicle. When you pass a parked vehicle, leave plenty of room. Remember people step out from in front of parked cars, or open doors. The further out from the obstruction you are, the better you can see round it.

The pupil will find it difficult to judge the distance from the parked car. You will have to help him with this.

At this stage, you will have to help him judge if it is safe to pass stationary vehicles when there are other cars coming in the opposite direction. This is called 'meeting' another vehicle. It is too early to go into details with the pupil at this stage about meeting other vehicles safely, but you will be explaining it in a later lesson (page 156). He will rely on you to judge this for him at the moment.

Remember, if there is any doubt in your mind then get him to stop. It is always good practice for moving away!

There is more information concerning the problems that can arise when overtaking on pages 101 and 189.

Traffic lights (See also page 63 for sequence of lights)

When you reach traffic lights, the correct procedure for the pupil is as follows:

Straight on at lights (See Fig. 10)
Always keep in the left lane unless the road markings show otherwise. Remember you must always keep to the left in normal driving.

If you were on the right you would find that when you moved

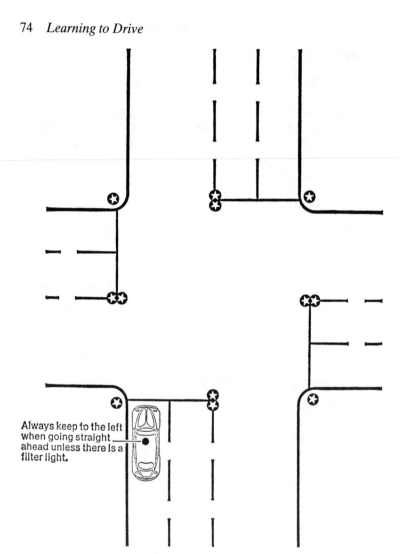

Always keep to the left when going straight ahead unless there is a filter light.

Fig. 10 Traffic lights: position when going straight on.

away from the lights you would be stuck out in the middle of the road with vehicles on your left who are going straight on.

Usually the only exception to this rule is when there is a filter light to the left. There should always be road markings in these circumstances.

Turning left at lights   (See Fig. 11)

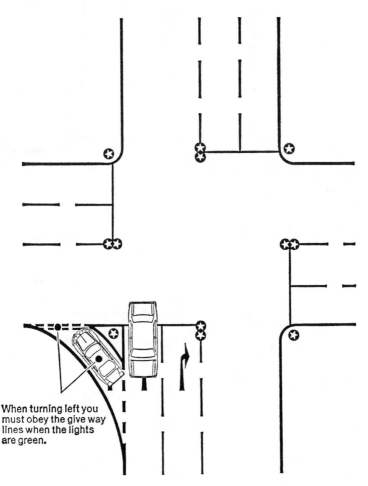

When turning left you must obey the give way lines when the lights are green.

Fig. 11   Traffic lights with slip road.

Always keep in the left lane and watch out for filter lights. Slip roads should be taken where possible but watch for the give way lines at the junction with the other road. (You must look RIGHT, LEFT AND RIGHT AGAIN before emerging.)

Care must be taken not to confuse some junctions which appear to have slip roads which are, in fact, service roads. These service roads should not normally be taken as they are only for parking. Usually slip roads are marked with arrows.

Turning right at lights   (See Figs 12 and 13)
Practise the usual procedure of mirror, signal, position and gears as you approach the lights, getting into the right lane as soon as possible.

When the lights are green, it is usual to move as far forward as possible, passing the cars that are turning right from the opposite direction on your right. Turn the wheel to the right as you stop. When the road is clear, continue round the corner. Do not block the road if there are other cars in front of you.

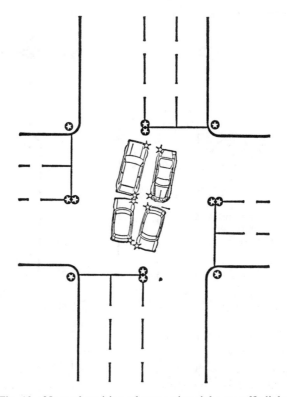

Fig. 12   Normal position when turning right at traffic lights.

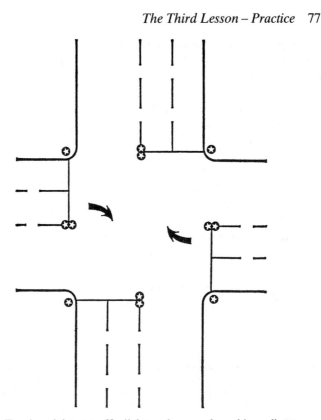

Fig. 13 Turning right at traffic lights, when road markings dictate you should pass other right turning vehicles on your left.

There are some junctions controlled by traffic lights that have road markings showing that you should turn in front of the opposite traffic (Fig. 13). In other words, pass the traffic that is turning right from the opposite direction on your LEFT. If you follow the road markings there should be no problems as long as you look out for oncoming traffic, remembering that this traffic could be obscured by the oncoming traffic waiting to turn right.

This latter type of junction often causes much confusion to the pupil, so try to find one or two of this type to practise at in the later lessons. They are also quite a problem for the instructor, because sitting on the near side your vision is often obscured.

General points regarding traffic lights

If you have to stop at the lights, it is better to wait in 1st gear with the clutch kept fully depressed. You are then ready to move away as soon as the lights change. You must have your hand brake on.

You may become nervous at traffic lights because of the pressure of traffic, and, if stopped, the worry of moving away in time. This is why it is better to be ready to move away with first gear selected. This does not harm the clutch mechanism as long as your foot is kept right down on the clutch. If the car is in neutral while you wait, you are more likely to panic when the lights change. The wrong gear is selected, or there is difficulty selecting 1st gear, by which time the lights have changed again.

It makes no difference in the driving test whether the car is in 1st gear or neutral, but what is important is that you keep as calm as possible and are ready to move when the lights change.

The hand brake must be applied as soon as the car stops at the lights. When turning right and it is necessary to wait at the centre of the junction for the road to clear, it is not essential to apply the hand brake unless on a hill.

If the pupil stalls the engine at the lights, do not rush him. Give clear, unhurried instructions in your normal voice: 'Hand brake on, into neutral, start the engine, clutch down, select 1st gear, control the clutch,' and so on. Do not worry too much about the cars waiting behind you. The pupil can only do things at his own speed. Remember, always make him apply the hand brake and put the gear into neutral if the engine is stalled. Not only is it safer, but it will give him a second or two to collect his thoughts. Stalling the engine does not matter, it is what he does afterwards that is important.

In the earlier lessons you can help him by anticipating the change of lights. When you know that the lights are about to change (by seeing the opposite lights changing), tell the pupil to accelerate slightly and to start bringing up the clutch. This can save a few seconds.

Always approach green lights at between 15 to 20 miles per hour, in 3rd gear, or more slowly, of course, according to the traffic conditions, because they are potentially dangerous crossroads.

Beware of other vehicles suddenly turning in front or across you. Never presume that you have the right of way and take the green light for granted. People do 'jump' lights occasionally!

Be ready for pedestrians suddenly crossing.

You must also be ready for the lights to change to amber

(which means **stop**!) This means you must be going slow enough to stop.

Here the instructor must be ready to anticipate the pupil. It is up to you to decide, on the spur of the moment, whether he should stop or go on if the lights change to amber. If you consider that you are too close then tell him to continue. Be definite because there must be no confusion. Beware of him suddenly slamming his foot on the brake, because it has been known for a pupil to stop dead at the lights when everyone presumed he was going to continue.

There is usually a point some metres (yards) before the lights when the instructor can say 'Carry on through the lights even if they change'. It is up to you to judge this.

If the lights change to amber as you approach it is not necessary to change down to 2nd gear before you stop, unless there is a possibility of the lights changing to green before you get there.

Roundabouts

Most learners find roundabouts extremely confusing, so it is a good idea if the method of negotiating them is explained before one is met.

It is very important to give the pupil clear direction instructions when approaching roundabouts.

Turning left at roundabouts (See Fig. 14)

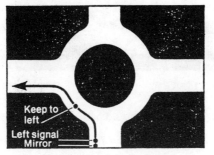

Fig. 14 Turning left at roundabouts.

Your instruction to the pupil should be:

I want you to turn left at the roundabout, that is to take the first exit road.

1.   *Look in mirror.*
2.   *Signal intention to turn left.*
3.   *Keep to the left.*
4.   *Slow down on brake.*
5.   *Change to 2nd gear just before the roundabout (about 6 metres (6–7 yards)).*
6.   *As you approach, look to the right (also looking where you are going!).*
7a. *If the road is clear from the right, continue into the roundabout, keeping to the left.*
7b. *If the road is not clear, STOP! Then continue when it is safe, keeping to the left.*

Always give way to traffic coming from the right. If there is any doubt as to which way the traffic is going, then stop. Remember vehicles often enter roundabouts very quickly, so although the road could appear empty one second, it could be busy the next.

Straight on at roundabouts (2nd exit road)   (See Fig. 15)

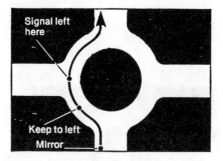

Fig. 15   Going straight on at roundabouts.

Your instruction to the pupil should be:

I want you to continue straight on at the roundabout, that is to take the second exit road.

1.   *Look in the mirror.*
2.   *DO NOT SIGNAL.*
3.   *Keep to the left.*
4.   *Slow down on the brake.*

5. *Change to 2nd gear just before the roundabout.*
6. *As you approach, look to the right (also looking where you are going).*
7a. *If the road is clear, continue on to the roundabout, keeping to the left.*
7b. *If it is not clear, stop. Continue when it is safe, keeping to the left.*
8. *When you are level with the first road, signal left.*
9. *Continue out of the roundabout into the 2nd road, still keeping to the left.*

Turning right at roundabouts (3rd or 4th exit road)   (See Fig. 16)

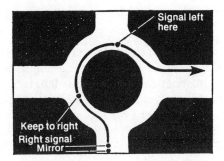

Fig. 16 Turning right at roundabouts.

Your instruction to the pupil should be:

I want you to turn right at the roundabout, that is take the 3rd (or 4th) turning.

1. *Check mirror.*
2. *Signal right and if safe to do so.*
3. *Move into the correct position (just to the left of the centre of the road, or into the righthand lane if marked).*
4. *Slow down on brake.*
5. *Change to 2nd gear just before the roundabout.*
6. *As you approach look to the right (also looking where you are going).*
7. *If the road is clear, continue into the roundabout keeping to the right (as near to the centre of the roundabout as possible). Keep the right indicator going.*

7b. *If it is not clear, stop. Continue when it is safe, keeping to the right.*

8. *When you get level with the 2nd road (the 3rd if you are taking the 4th), signal left.*

9. *Check mirror and to your left.*

10. *Continue out of roundabout into the 3rd (4th) road, keeping to the LEFT.*

Very often the pupil has no difficulty in understanding the procedure when it is explained but gets confused at the actual roundabout. Be ready to help the pupil on the first few roundabouts and you will find that he will soon gain confidence.

General points regarding roundabouts

Gear changing
When actually negotiating the roundabout, it is better not to change gear because both hands are needed for steering. However, if you are on a large roundabout and have moved off in 1st gear, it may be necessary to change into 2nd gear. The best time to change gear is when you have set the steering on a course round the curve of the roundabout. Although you won't be travelling in a straight line, the wheel is at least held in one position. Provided that the gear change is completed before the need to turn the wheel back to the left, it is quite safe.

Never change gear when you have to change direction.

Moving off
When you have to stop before entering a roundabout, be ready to move away as soon as possible because the traffic on roundabouts is often fast moving, and when there is an opportunity to move, you must be ready to take it.

Speed when approaching
Always approach roundabouts slowly, because although it may look clear when you are 22 metres (25 yards) from the roundabout, the situation can change very quickly. Other vehicles often move quickly into roundabouts, so you must be ready to give way at the last moment.

Always ensure that you look where you are going, both when approaching the roundabout and when negotiating it. Very often you are so busy looking for traffic coming from the right that the road in front is forgotten.

Mini-roundabouts   (See Fig 17)

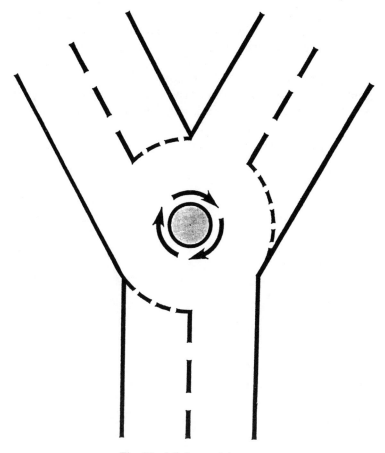

Fig. 17   Mini-roundabout.

These are usually encountered as busy road junctions and therefore often have only three exit roads. Mini-roundabouts help to keep the traffic moving provided that everybody uses them correctly. Unfortunately this is not always the case; so beware of them.

The same rules apply at a mini-roundabout as at any other

roundabout, i.e. you must give way to traffic approaching from your right. They are usually well marked with warning signs but be especially careful that the vehicles coming from the left do give way to you. Never presume that you are going to be given the right of way. Remember also that large vehicles may have difficulty in negotiating the roundabout and require plenty of room.

Always negotiate these mini-roundabouts very slowly, in 2nd or 1st gear.

One of the problems here is that other motorists tend to 'nip' in front of the learner driver, often causing very dangerous situations. As long as you are aware of the problem you can act accordingly. If there is any doubt, stop at the broken white line.

The Fourth Lesson – Preparation

Driving on hills

The response and effect of the controls is very different depending on whether the car is being driven uphill, downhill or on the level. It is important to understand why and how the car responds differently on hills, otherwise it is impossible to keep full control of the car at all times.

When you practised the hill start you would have noticed that, compared with moving off on the level, more acceleration was needed to move the car away from a stationary position. Once having moved off you then had to increase the speed of the car considerably more than you would have done on level ground before you could change up to a higher gear. This was to allow for the pull of gravity on the car which has the effect of slowing the car down when the clutch is depressed.

The response and effect of the controls differ when driving up- or downhill, compared with driving on the level, in the following ways:

Driving uphill

1. More acceleration is needed to increase the speed of the car. The use of a low gear will help to pull the car up a hill.
2. The car will slow down more quickly when the brakes are applied and therefore less, and slightly later braking, is necessary.
3. When the pressure is reduced on the accelerator the car will

slow down more quickly. Always be ready to change down to a lower gear.

4. The car will slow down when the clutch is depressed therefore care must be taken to allow more road speed before changing up gear.

5. When you are stopping, less pressure is needed on the brake but the hand brake must be used immediately after stopping to avoid the car rolling back. The brake can be used slightly later when stopping.

Driving downhill

1. It is more difficult for the brakes to slow the car down when driving downhill, therefore early use of the brake is essential.

2. In a high gear the engine will not slow the car down as effectively when the pressure is lifted off the accelerator as when travelling uphill. In low gear the engine will help to keep a check on the speed of the car but will not actually slow the car down.

3. When the clutch is depressed the car will gain speed. This makes gear changing more difficult, therefore it is important to be in the correct gear when you begin the descent. The use of the brakes when you are de-clutching is essential.

4. Because of the effect of these three points, extreme care must be taken when approaching corners. Early use of the brakes and correct gear changing are essential when approaching bends and junctions downhill to avoid loss of control.

General hints regarding hills

When you are approaching a hill you must decide how steep and how long it is to enable you to adjust the speed of the car and to choose the correct gear. You must also take into consideration other factors, for example, your view ahead could be affected if there is a bend or junction on the hill. Hills vary to a great extent making it impossible to generalise on the gear that you should engage and at what speed you should travel. It is safe to say that for uphill gradients you will need to be accelerating as you approach and for downhill gradients you will need to be slowing down by easing your foot off the accelerator and possibly using the brakes, depending upon how steep the hill is. The exact gear that you choose will also depend on the gradient and problems of the particular hill. The steeper the hill, the lower the gear, irrespective of whether you are travelling uphill or downhill.

Other vehicles on hills

It is important to remember that other drivers experience the same problems as you when ascending or descending a hill, therefore you must allow for this. When following a large vehicle up a hill you should stay further back to allow room to take action if it slows down or even stops. With a heavy load it is difficult for the driver of a large vehicle to keep sufficient road speed to climb a steep hill and gear changing is very difficult in these conditions.

Overtaking can be more hazardous because you need more speed when going uphill and therefore more time to complete the manoeuvre. When overtaking uphill you must also take into account the fact that the vehicle coming downhill is often travelling much more quickly than you realise. It takes more time for these vehicles to slow down and it is equally more difficult for you to accelerate out of trouble.

Extreme care must be taken when overtaking downhill also, because it then takes more time for you to slow down and, of course, it is more difficult for the vehicle coming uphill towards you to increase speed if necessary.

In general, then, it is more difficult to judge the speeds of others and control the vehicle when you are on a hill. You must try not to cause inconvenience to other road users, especially when you are meeting or crossing their path. (See pages 156–9.) When you are emerging from a junction, try not to balk other vehicles which are coming up the hill. This is particularly important when you are turning right on to the incline at a 'T' junction because you first have to cross the vehicles coming down the hill and then move into the stream of slow moving vehicles going up the hill. If you drive courteously, you are more likely to drive safely.

Warning signs for hills

On the steeper and larger types of hills there are usually warning signs as you approach. These signs give you valuable information as to how steep the hill is, whether it is uphill or downhill and sometimes, advise you to engage a low gear. Look for the signs because they are a great help. They are triangular in shape with a red border and the gradient of the hill is usually written as a percentage in black lettering above an upward or downward slope. The higher the percentage, the steeper the hill (e.g. 20% = 1:5, 10% = 1:10).

Many hills do not have warning signs therefore you must look well ahead so that you can anticipate the possible dangers and approach at the correct speed in the correct gear.

Notes for the instructor

Most learners do not realise that they are on a hill, especially in the early lessons. You must get the pupil to notice the different gradients and to drive accordingly because if he approaches a junction without realising that he is going downhill, it could cause a very dangerous situation. (See page 86.)

It is a good idea to let the pupil experiment with the brake, accelerator and clutch on both uphill and downhill gradients. This will give him a chance to feel the different response and effect of the controls. This practice should be done on quiet roads without causing any danger to other road users.

Many learners become confused about using the gears correctly on hills. You will probably find that he will want to change down gears even where it is not necessary or will change too early or too late. Only experience through practice will help the pupil to understand the many different types of hill and it is not until he has a real feel for the car and the relative engine and road speeds in each gear that he will become competent at driving up or down hills.

The Fourth Lesson – Practice

Duration of lesson one hour

In this lesson we will be covering crossroads and turning in the road (often called the 3-point turn).

As with the previous lessons, work out a route before the lesson. Include all the things you practised in the earlier lesson, e.g. traffic lights, roundabouts, left and right turns, etc.

When driving yourself between the pupil's lessons, keep an eye open for roads in your local area which could be suitable for the lesson. You can usually find suitable roads in which manoeuvres such as turning in the road and reverse can be done not too far from your home.

Before you start the lesson, explain crossroads to your pupil:

Crossroads (See Fig. 18)

There are several different types of crossroads; some where you have the right of way, some where you must give way, and others where there is no right of way. There are two things in common with all types of crossroads. They are all dangerous, and you must LOOK RIGHT, LEFT AND RIGHT AGAIN before you emerge. Remember that even at a crossroads where you have the right of way, there is nothing to stop another vehicle ignoring the signs, so always look!

Crossroads where you have the right of way (See Fig. 18)
These are crossroads where the GIVE WAY or STOP signs are for traffic approaching from the right or left of you, with no markings

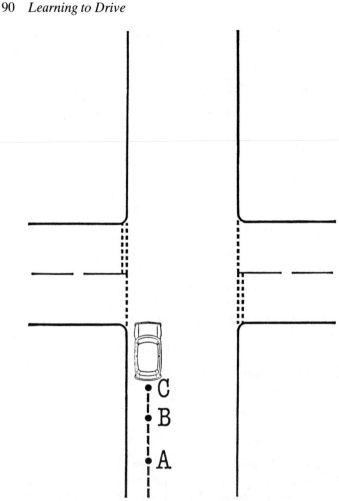

Fig. 18   Crossroads   *On the major road:* when you have the right of way you must still look right, left and right again before you reach the crossing. As you approach the crossroad you must look right at 'A' on the diagram. Look left at 'B' and right again at 'C'. This will enable you to have the best possible view of the side roads. The speed at which you approach the crossroads depends upon the width of road that you are on and your view of the other road.

On the minor road: look right, left and right again before emerging. You must be travelling at a slow enough speed to be able to stop at the broken white lines (the use of 1st gear is often necessary).

across the road on which you are travelling. The speed at which you approach this type of crossroad depends on the type and width of the road that you are on, and the conditions prevailing at the time. A general rule is the smaller the road you are on, the slower you must approach the crossroads, but you must look right, left and right again before you enter the junction. If you are on a busy, wide main road and there are no obstructions blocking your view of the crossroad, then you need not slow down very much. Just to come off the accelerator and cover the brake is often sufficient, without even changing gear.

The important thing is that you start looking RIGHT early, (Position A in Fig. 18), so that you have time to then look LEFT and RIGHT again before you reach the crossroads. If you leave it too late to look RIGHT, you will have passed the crossroads before you have completed looking LEFT and RIGHT again.

You will find that the first look RIGHT will give you only a limited view of the road, but this is sufficient to see if anybody is actually about to drive into the main road. When you look left, you will be that much nearer the crossroad, and will therefore be able to see quite a long way down to your left (Position B), and when you look right again (Position C), you should be able to see far enough down the road to your right to be sure it is safe. By this time, provided you have not taken too long in looking, you should still be a metre (yard) or two from the junction. You can then go back on the accelerator again if it is safe.

The wider the road you are on, the earlier and easier you can see down the side-roads. With more experience, you will be able to ascertain the speed at which another car is approaching the GIVE WAY sign, and act accordingly. The smaller and narrower the road that you are on, the more you have to slow down when approaching the crossroads, and of course this could mean changing down to 3rd or 2nd gear.

In the diagram, the roads are all equal width and quite small. Although you have the right of way, your vision is probably obscured by hedges or fences. The traffic coming from the right or left may not treat the road that you are on as being very important and so they may not take so much care in giving way. This is where most accidents happen.

You must slow down sufficiently to be able to see and act in case of an emergency. You cannot look to the right as early as in the wider roads, because your vision will be obscured, so you must slow down enough to look RIGHT, LEFT and RIGHT AGAIN before emerging into the junction. If there are parked cars, then you will have to slow down even more. Whether you use 3rd or 2nd gear depends on your speed. It is important at these crossroads to remember the traffic behind you. You must look in your mirror when you approach, before you slow down, and give a slowing down signal if necessary. Once you have satisfied yourself that it is safe, then increase your speed by getting back on the accelerator again. You do not want to waste unnecessary time and hold up other traffic at the crossroads so do not dawdle once past the crossroad.

Having just explained the two extremes of crossroads where the pupil has the right of way, you must help him to judge his speed at the different types of crossroads that fall between the two extremes.

Make sure that he really does look properly. Sometimes the pupil goes through the motions of looking, but he does not really see anything.

Also make sure that he does not look for too long and forgets to look where he is going.

Crossroads where you must give way

These are crossroads where the GIVE WAY or STOP sign is across your path at the end of the road.

At the give way sign (broken double white lines) you must give way to any traffic on the other road, but you do not have to stop, provided that you look RIGHT, LEFT and RIGHT AGAIN, and have satisfied yourself that it is safe to continue before you emerge. This means that you must be going slowly enough to look properly and stop, if you have to before you cross the white lines.

Very often at crossroads, as with normal road junctions, it is impossible to see properly unless you do stop, so if there is any doubt at all in your mind then STOP.

The best way to judge if you should stop or not is to look to the right some 15 metres (16 yards) before the junction. If you can see 20–30 metres (25–35 yards) down the road then you may be able to continue without stopping, provided that you look left and you can see far enough to the left. If you cannot see enough at this stage, or if the road is not clear then stop. If you do decide to continue, make sure that you look right again before you enter the other road. IF IN DOUBT STOP!

You will not find many junctions of this type, where it is not necessary to stop.

Crossroads where there is no right of way
These are crossroads where there are no road markings or signs, except perhaps a SLOW sign painted on the road as you approach.

They are usually on minor roads and are extremely dangerous. The trouble is that drivers sometimes disregard these crossroads altogether because they are on such small roads, and drive across them at great speed.

You must slow right down, change to 2nd or even 1st gear, and look RIGHT, LEFT and RIGHT AGAIN before emerging. Sometimes you may even have to stop if your vision is obscured by a fence or parked vehicle, etc.

These then are the different types of crossroads. Remember, the smaller the road that you are on, the more dangerous the crossroads and where there is no right of way, it means you must be ready to give way.

Get as much practice on crossroads as possible. Especially try to find one or two unmarked crossroads, as the examiner in the driving test is almost certain to take you across one.

Start Lesson 4 in the same road as the other lessons. Go through the same routine as before and practise all the things done in the previous lessons. If anything needs more practice, go over it a few times.

Sometimes at this stage of driving, you go through a period of 'relapse'. You do not appear to be driving as well as in the previous lessons. No need to worry about this because there could be many reasons for it.

Often it is because you become a little careless in the actual control of the car, i.e. the use of the clutch, etc. The control of the clutch must be thought about the whole time. It will be a very long time before the clutch control becomes 'second nature'. It can also appear that you are not doing so well because more difficult manoeuvres and situations are being attempted and mistakes are being made, although, in fact, you are advancing well.

Continue the pupil round your route instructing him all the time and commenting on mistakes.

If anything needs explaining in any detail, then instruct him to stop the car in a convenient place and explain it while parked. Do not expect him to be listening intently to you and concentrating on the road at the same time. Take him across a few crossroads of different types, and remember that most of the lesson should be on the smaller types of roads with plenty of right and left turns.

Suitable road for practising turning in road by using forward and reverse gears (3-point turn)

To do the turn in the road you will need a suitable road where it is reasonably quiet. The width of the road is important.   ·

A suitable road would be one measuring approximately 7 metres (8 yards) in width, from kerb to kerb. To avoid the necessity of measuring it you could try a turn in the road yourself in a road which looks appropriate.

If you accomplish this without difficulty then it should prove a good spot for the pupil to practise. If you have to struggle, then it will probably be too narrow for the learner. A road wide enough for a 'U' turn is too wide.

When he is first practising turning in the road, it is better for there to be only a slight camber on the road, but later, try to find roads with quite steep cambers. He must practise on all types.

When you reach the road in which you have planned to practise the 3-point turn, tell him to stop on the left, switch the engine off and explain the manoeuvre to him:

Turning in the road, using forward and reverse gears (3-point turn)

The idea of the 3-point turn is to turn the car round and face it in the opposite direction by moving (A) forward across the road to the right, (B) reverse across the road to the left and then (C) forward again across the road to finish in a parking position on the opposite side of the road. (See Fig. 19.)

The reason for this manoeuvre is to show the examiner in the driving test that you have co-ordinated use of all of the major controls on the car as well as the capability of employing observation for safety within a limited space. The limited space is the road

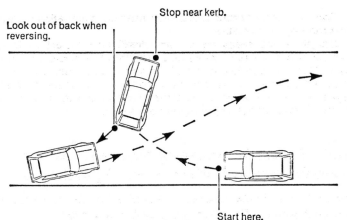

Fig. 19 3-point turn.

between the two kerbs and it is important that you do not touch either kerb. It is not essential that the manoeuvre is completed in three movements of the vehicle, but the examiner will expect you to keep the car under control, to use reasonable accuracy and to maintain proper observation. The vital thing is that you must move the car very slowly. There is only one way of doing this; that is, by controlling the clutch.

When you have put the car into 1st gear and have the correct amount of acceleration, you lift the clutch to the 'biting point', and as the car begins to move forward, hold your foot in that position. The car will then move very slowly to give you time to turn the wheel as hard as possible to the right. If you feel that you are going too fast, then put the clutch down a fraction. If you stop too early, lift the clutch a fraction, but do not alter the position of the accelerator. Most roads have a camber (a slope down both sides to allow water to drain off), so as you pass the centre of the road, the car starts to go downhill. At this point, put your clutch down and let the car roll slowly towards the kerb. Just before you reach the kerb, brake very gently to stop the car. It is a good idea to turn the wheel at least once in the opposite direction (to the left), just before you stop. This straightens the front wheels and saves having to turn the steering wheel so much while reversing.

Explain the first part of the manoeuvre before he starts to practise it, then explain the reversing when he has stopped on the other side of the road. He will not remember the reversing part anyway, if you tell him too much before you start. You must dictate every move to him throughout the manoeuvre.

Do the manoeuvre very slowly. The difficult part is when you have passed the centre of the road and are nearing the other kerb. Be ready to stop if necessary. Make sure you put the clutch down at the right time (i.e. just past the centre of the road). Some roads have very little camber, and it is possible for the car to stop when the clutch is depressed. If this happens just keep accelerating slightly and gently bring the clutch up again. Far better to go too slowly or to stop altogether than to go too fast.

It is up to the instructor to make sure that it is safe, because although you will make the pupil look round before he moves away, something could easily appear in the road in the meantime.

If, after you reach the other side of the road, before you start the reverse part of the manoeuvre, a vehicle approaches, then wave him on if it is safe to do so. There is no point in holding up other traffic unnecessarily.

Start the engine and we will practise it.

(Remember, it is always the same routine.)

1. *Depress the clutch.*
2. *Select 1st gear.*
3. *Find correct amount of acceleration.*
4. *Lift clutch slowly until you find the biting point.*
5. *Look in mirror and OVER RIGHT SHOULDER, and if safe (no signal necessary) . . .*
6. *Release handbrake, replacing hands on wheel.*
7. *Start lifting the clutch further until the car begins to move forward. (Quick look over right shoulder again.)*
8. *As the car moves forward keep the clutch in that position.*
9. *Turn the wheel as quickly as possible to the right until the wheel will go no further.*
10. *Having turned the wheel to its full extent, keep control of the clutch until you are just over the centre of the road, then . . .*
11. *Depress the clutch.*
12. *Off the accelerator, cover the brake, and just before you reach the kerb . . .*
13. *Turn the wheel quickly to the left at least once.*

14.   Brake slightly to stop just before the kerb.
15.   Hand brake on.
16.   Gear into reverse.

It is very difficult for the pupil to judge his distance from the kerb, so you must tell him when to brake until he has practised it a few times. Sometimes he may put his foot on the accelerator instead of the brake. Watch out for this because it causes panic.

You must, of course, show him where reverse gear is. Once he is in reverse gear tell him to keep his foot right down on the clutch while you explain the next part of the manoeuvre!

Now we have to reverse across the road, turning the wheel as hard as possible to the left, but remember, we are on a hill here so a hill start is necessary. It is important that when the change of sound or 'biting point' is reached and the hand brake released, the car does not move, because before the car moves, you must remove your hand from the hand brake on to the wheel and look RIGHT and LEFT to make sure it is safe to proceed. This is where good clutch control is so important.

We will now practise it.

(The clutch is still depressed and reverse gear is engaged.)

1.   Find correct accleration. (Better to have too much than not enough.)
2.   Start lifting the clutch until the change of sound is heard, then hold it there. The car should not move at this stage.
3.   Look RIGHT and LEFT. If safe . . .
4.   Release hand brake, replacing hand on wheel. Look RIGHT and LEFT AGAIN . . .
5.   If safe, lift clutch slightly until car begins to move, and then hold it there.
6.   Keeping the clutch controlled, turn the wheel hard and quickly to the left, looking where you are going over your left shoulder at the same time.
7.   Having turned the wheel to its fullest extent, keep control of the clutch until you are just over the crown of the road, then . . .
8.   Depress clutch.
9.   Off the accelerator, cover the brake and look over right shoulder so that you can see where you are in relation to the kerb . . .

10.   Turn the wheel quickly at least once to the right.
11.   Brake slightly to stop just before the kerb.
12.   Hand brake on.
13.   Select 1st gear.

The reason for looking over the left shoulder first and then the right shoulder is that for the first half of the road, the left shoulder is nearer the kerb and therefore the easiest to look over. For the other half, it is easiest to see the kerb by looking over the right shoulder.

If this is found particularly difficult, then it would suffice to just look over the left shoulder the whole way. The important thing is that you look where you are going when reversing. So many learners look out to the front when reversing, with disastrous consequences. Look out for trees and lamp-posts when reversing. You must know if there is an obstruction behind you.

Remember to take just as much time over the last part of the manoeuvre. Just as much control is needed. We are still on a hill so clutch control is again very important, so that you do not move until the hand brake is released, both hands are on the wheel and you have looked right and left.

Clutch is still depressed and 1st gear engaged.

1.   Find correct acceleration.
2.   Start lifting the clutch until the change of sound is heard, then hold it there.
3.   Look RIGHT and LEFT. If safe . . .
4.   Release hand brake, replacing hand on wheel. Look right and left again.
5.   If safe, lift clutch slightly until car starts to move, then hold it there.
6.   Keeping the clutch controlled turn the wheel to the right sufficiently to get the car round into a parking position on the lefthand side of the road.
7.   Still controlling the clutch, stop the car with gentle application of the brake.
8.   Hand brake on.
9.   Gear into neutral.
This completes the turn in the road.

Go over any points that you feel need explaining and try the turn again. Do not expect him to accomplish it more quickly the second time. You will also have to dictate it again, stage by stage, until he is more experienced.

When the second turn is completed make it the last one for this lesson to avoid putting the pupil under too much strain.

Four common faults to look for when turning in the road

1. Not turning the wheel soon or quickly enough. The wheel should be turned on full lock within the first 1 or 2 metres (1–2 yards) of moving off. Ensure that you do not try to turn the wheel while the car is stationary.
2. Moving off in reverse, or last turn before you are ready. It is vital that both hands are on the wheel and that you have looked both ways before moving off.
3. Not looking where you are going while reversing.
4. Forgetting which way to turn the wheel while reversing. This fault is very common.

   Practice will cure it but at first it is best to remind him before he starts moving if there is any doubt.

Never stop to do a turn in the road where there is a tree or lamp-post just in front of you because when you reverse back across the road, it will be directly behind you.

Observation on this manoeuvre is most important, so make sure you look in all directions before moving off.

Every lesson from now on should include at least one turn in the road. It never has to be done quickly. Always do it in your own time. Eventually you will be able to do it without having each stage dictated to you, but this might take anything between 10 and 20 attempts at it. Don't forget to re-fasten your seat belts if they are removed for the manoeuvre.

The Fifth Lesson – Preparation

Keeping a safe distance behind other vehicles

When you are driving behind other vehicles you must give yourself time and space to stop. Generally speaking, you should be at least far enough behind the vehicle in front to allow for the normal stopping distances (which are given below) when you are driving on good road surfaces and in good weather conditions. As the road surfaces get worse and the weather deteriorates, so the distance must be lengthened. It takes at least twice as long to stop on wet roads and up to ten times as long in icy conditions.

Larger vehicles create more problems for you because of the lack of visibility when you follow them. Leave a greater distance between yourself and the large vehicle so that you can see to the left of the vehicle as well as to the right.

It is not always possible to keep as far back as you might like when following vehicles at slow speeds because of the available space and amount of traffic in the road. You will have to use your common sense in these situations and stay as far back as you can without wasting too much valuable road space. If you stay too far back, the car behind will only overtake you, defeating the object.

The most important thing is to be looking well ahead, not just at the vehicle in front, but look well down the road to give yourself time to act.

It is difficult for the inexperienced driver to judge the stopping distance and the distance between you and the car in front. A rough guide is to keep about one metre (1 yard) for every mph of your speed behind the vehicle you are following.

Stopping distances in good conditions

20 mph	12 metres (13 yards)
30 mph	23 metres (25 yards)
40 mph	37 metres (40 yards)
50 mph	53 metres (58 yards)
60 mph	73 metres (80 yards)
70 mph	96 metres (105 yards)

Overtaking moving vehicles (See Fig. 20)

This can be one of the most dangerous manoeuvres when driving. More people are killed and injured while overtaking therefore you must consider several important points:

1. Is the available road wide enough for overtaking?
2. Am I sure that I am not going to endanger or inconvenience any other road users by overtaking?
3. Is this a safe place to overtake? (The *Highway Code* gives many places at which it is not safe to overtake. You should learn these.)
4. Is the vehicle that is to be overtaken travelling at a constant speed and direction and is it likely to keep doing so while it is overtaken?
5. Have I got enough speed and power to overtake the vehicle safely?
6. Can I gauge the length of the other vehicle?

If you can answer yes to all the above questions, you can then go through the procedure of overtaking which includes the routine of MIRROR, SIGNAL and MANOEUVRE.

Procedure for overtaking
1. Position the car safely where you can see ahead. You should be far enough behind the vehicle you are going to overtake to be able to see round it without having to pull out. The larger the vehicle, the further back you have to be. If you decide it is safe ahead to overtake:
2. Select the correct gear for the speed and power that you will need.
3. Look in the mirror. If safe . . .

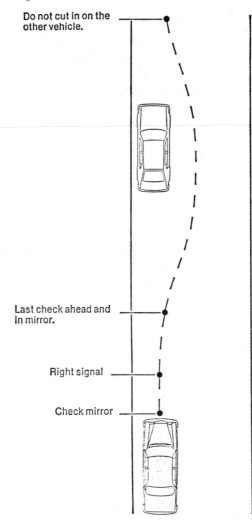

Do not cut in on the other vehicle.

Last check ahead and in mirror.

Right signal

Check mirror

Fig. 20   Overtaking moving vehicles.

4.   Signal right with the indicator.
5.   Check again ahead and behind (in mirror) and if still safe . . .
6.   Overtake as quickly as possible without getting too close to the vehicle you are overtaking.
7.   Pull in gently once you are well clear of the overtaken vehicle.

When you are deciding if it is safe ahead you must bear in mind that it is impossible to judge the accurate speed of oncoming traffic so if there is any doubt in your mind you must wait. You must also look for turnings and openings on the righthand side of the road ahead of where you are going to overtake because if a car emerges from one of these turnings as you are overtaking you could be in trouble.

When you select the correct gear for overtaking you must know at what speed you are travelling and then judge the correct amount of acceleration that you will need. Usually you will either change down a gear, or stay in the gear you are in, depending upon your road speed. With experience you will get to know the best gear for the relative speed and power needed. This differs greatly from one car to another. Remember that you will have to accelerate slightly to achieve a smooth gear change when you change down to a lower gear in these circumstances. (See page 61.)

Do not 'cut in' on the other vehicle after overtaking. Leave plenty of room because the other vehicle is still moving and it will be difficult to judge your distance.

Golden rules when overtaking

Make sure it is safe, decide early, overtake quickly when you have decided and get back into the correct position on the left of the road as soon and safely as possible. Remember that the dangerous time is when you are on the wrong side of the road and therefore on collision course with oncoming traffic, so the more quickly you get past the other vehicle and on to the correct side of the road the better.

Overtaking stationary vehicles

Most of the rules apply as when you are overtaking a moving vehicle. There are, however, other important factors to be taken into consideration which are fully explained on pages 73 and 156.

Notes for the instructor

It is difficult to practise overtaking moving vehicles with the pupil because the opportunity does not occur very often. There will, however, be times when slow moving vehicles such as milk floats, dust carts and road sweeping lorries can be overtaken by the pupil. The technique of overtaking, although at a slow speed, can be taught when these opportunities do arise.

Later, when the pupil drives on the main roads for longer periods, overtaking can be practised at higher speeds. Don't forget though, that there is the added problem that from the position in which you are sitting, it is difficult for you to see and be sure that the road ahead is safe for overtaking. Do not just rely on the pupil's judgement until you are positive that he is capable of judging correctly. This could be a long time away! If in doubt, do not let him overtake.

There will be plenty of opportunities for the pupil to practise overtaking stationary vehicles and other obstructions. If the overtaking sequence can be explained and related to overtaking moving vehicles it will help him for the future. (Also see pages 73 and 156.)

The Fifth Lesson – Practice

Duration of lesson one and a half hours

On this lesson we will be practising the reverse. When planning your route, as well as finding suitable roads to practise all that has been learned in the previous lessons, you will have to find a junction where you can practise reversing round a corner.

Types of road for reversing   (See Fig. 21)

Try to find a kerb for reversing that curves round evenly. It does not matter how sharp the corner is because it is important to practise on all types of corners.

At first make sure that the road is flat for reversing. Later reversing can be practised on hills. Remember, you must always reverse out of a main road, not vice versa.

It is important to see for yourself at what point you turn the wheel in your car in relation to the kerb. Remember all cars differ slightly. With some cars, it is best to look out of the corner of the back window until the kerb nearly disappears, with some you have to wait until the kerb actually disappears, and with others, you have to wait until the kerb appears in the side window. Only by practising it yourself can you be sure.

Begin this lesson at the usual place. Practise everything from the previous lessons, including turning in the road.

Your instructor should still be talking you through everything, although by now you should be getting an idea of when to change gear. Change gear when you think you should without necessarily

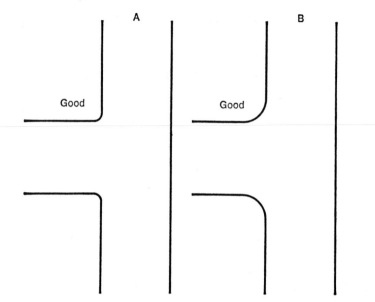

Fig. 21 Types of roads for reversing.

waiting for your instructor to tell you. You will probably be able to tell when to change up gears better than when to change them down, because you should be beginning to hear the sound of the engine, especially in 1st and 2nd gear. Do not worry if you do not fully understand the gears yet. You soon will.

Still keep your route relatively simple for this lesson, mainly concentrating on your correct procedure, observation and positioning when turning. If you concentrate on this at this stage, it will pay dividends later. Keep busy roads to a minimum, although a little practice on these will do no harm. (Next lesson we will be going into some more difficult situations.)

Continue round your route until you find your suitable road for reversing. Then stop on the left BEFORE the turning at which the reverse is to be practised.

The reason for stopping before the turning is that on the driving test, the examiner will normally stop you in this position to explain that he wants you to do the reverse. He will then ask you to move

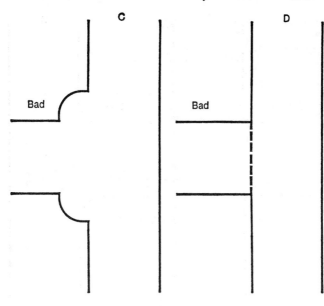

Fig. 22 Types of roads for not reversing.

forward to a suitable position just past the next turning on the left for reversing round the corner. This is so that you can see what type of corner you are going to reverse round, and so that you can get into the best possible position for the manoeuvre.

You should therefore get into the habit of doing this from the beginning. When you have stopped on the left before the turning, and have put the hand brake on and the gear into neutral, your instructor will say:

Reversing round a corner to the left   (See Fig. 23)

Now I want you to move forward to a position just past the next turning on the left, suitable to reverse the car into that road.
You should stop a few metres (yards) past the turning, not too close to the kerb (about half a metre (2 feet) from the kerb).

If you stop too close to the kerb, it will be difficult for you to reverse round the corner in the correct position. (You would have to

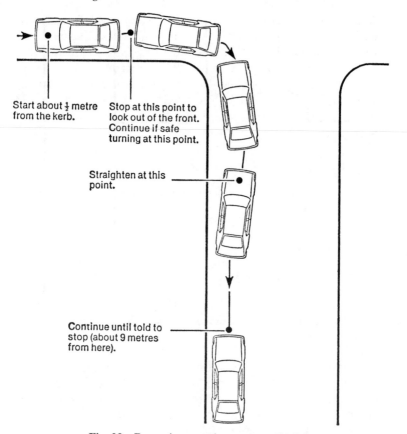

Start about ½ metre from the kerb.

Stop at this point to look out of the front. Continue if safe turning at this point.

Straighten at this point.

Continue until told to stop (about 9 metres from here).

Fig. 23   Reversing round a corner to the left.

turn too wide.) Before you move away from the parking position before the turning, make sure that you look in the mirror and over your right shoulder. Before you stop in the position for the reverse, make sure that you check the mirror. I mention this because it is easy to forget this while thinking about the reverse.

A signal before stopping, if necessary, must be given with the arm, because a left signal with the indicator would be too confusing to other road users, as you are near a left junction.

In your driving test you have to reverse the car round the corner and along the side road, keeping as close to the kerb as possible.

Make sure you twist your body round so that you can see easily out of the back of the car without straining your neck. You may feel uncomfortable in this position at first. It is permissible to release the seat belt for this manoeuvre but you must remember to fasten it afterwards. If you have trouble reaching the pedals in this position, then maybe your seat could be moved forward slightly or you could put a cushion behind your back. Unless you are far enough round, you will never be able to do the reverse properly.

There are two important points about the reverse.

1. Move the car very slowly
2. Turn the wheel at the correct place. The car is controlled very slowly by the clutch, with very little acceleration needed.

    The correct place to turn the wheel is when the kerb almost disappears from view when looking through the back window (this point could be different in your car). If you leave it later than that you will go too far out from the kerb at the corner. When you have reached the point to turn, you should stop (by depressing the clutch) because you must look out of the front of the car at this point to make sure that nobody is going to be endangered by the front of your car swinging out into the road as you turn the corner. (See Fig. 23.)

    Once you have turned the corner, look directly out of the back window to judge when to turn the wheel to the right to straighten it. The straightening of the wheel must be done very quickly with the car moving very slowly.

Position of hands while reversing

You will find it easier while reversing in a straight line to place your left arm on the back of the driving seat but while actually turning the corner, you will need both hands on the steering wheel to be able to turn properly. Once round the corner and having straightened up, you can then place the left arm on the back of the seat again. It is best to have your right hand at the top of the wheel when reversing with one hand.

Now we shall practise the reverse:
1. Clutch down.
2. Select reverse gear.

3. Move body round to the left into a better position to see out of the back of the car.
4. Find right amount of acceleration (very little). Do not alter the position of the accelerator once the correct amount of acceleration has been found.
5. Lift clutch slowly until you find the biting point then hold the clutch there.
6. Release hand brake. You will need only one hand at the top of the steering wheel at this stage. The other (left) hand can be rested on the back of your seat.
7. Look out through the front, side and back windows of the car to see if it is safe to move. Remember you must wait if anything is approaching and you must stop if anything comes at any stage of the manoeuvre. This includes pedestrians who may cross your path.
8. Look for the position of the kerb at which you are going to turn, and when this is reached . . .
9. STOP by depressing the clutch very slightly.
10. Look out of the front of the car, and if safe to continue, put both hands on the wheel.
11. Lift the clutch slightly and when the car starts to move, turn the wheel to the left sufficiently to get round the corner as parallel to the kerb as possible.
12. Look out of the back window until the road appears straight out of the back of the car, then . . .
13. Turn the wheel to the right quickly to straighten the car.

The important thing to note here is that the clutch is controlled well so that the car moves very slowly, but the wheel is turned quickly. It is better if the car is moving very slowly, even if it stops at this point, rather than moving too fast.

14. When the car is in a straight line parallel with the kerb, adjust the wheel very slightly and continue back in a straight line as close to the kerb as possible.

Make sure that you keep looking out of the back window. For some reason learners nearly always want to look out of the front at this stage. A quick glance out of the front to check on any possible dangers is all that is necessary after having turned the corner.

If it is easier you can take your left hand off the steering wheel, and adjust the steering if necessary with your right hand only, once you have straightened the wheel. If you do this it is better to hold the wheel at the top with your right hand.

Keep reversing until told to stop, then . . .

15. Clutch right down.
16. Brake gently if necessary (car will probably stop without the use of the brake unless on downhill slope).
17. Hand brake on.
18. Gear into neutral.

This completes the reverse.

Drive forward, turn left at the end of the road and stop in a good position to have another attempt.

Make sure that you look in the mirror and over your right shoulder before you move forward and that you look RIGHT, LEFT and RIGHT AGAIN before emerging into the road. Don't forget to fasten your seat belt if they were removed for the manoeuvre.

Have another attempt at it, going through every part. Make sure that you always do the reverse very slowly.

When you have completed the second reverse, continue on your route. As with the turn in the road, it is not a good idea to overdo this manoeuvre at first. Even if the second attempt was not very good, still continue on. You can practise the reverse again in the next lesson.

Common faults when reversing

1. Not getting into a proper position to see out of the back window.
2. Starting too close to the kerb, or getting too close as you drive back towards the corner.
3. Not observing enough (i.e. not looking in all directions before reversing, not looking out of the front of the car before turning, and not being ready to stop should a vehicle approach from another direction).

    It is not absolutely necessary that you stop just before you turn the corner. You could look out of the front of the car while you are still moving but often, by the time you look out of the back again you have driven into a bad position for the corner and finish up taking it too wide.

4. Going too fast while trying to straighten the wheel. Make sure you keep control of the clutch at this point.

5. Not turning the wheel quickly enough while straightening up.

6. Not looking out of the back of the car most of the time. The only time that you should not be looking out of the back is when you are looking for pedestrians and other vehicles.

   This is very important because if you look out of the front for more than a split second you could easily lose your sense of direction.

7. Over-steering when trying to keep parallel with the kerb.

8. Once the reverse is completed, make sure you look in the mirror and over your right shoulder before moving forward. Very often, you are still thinking about the reverse when you move off again.

   Sometimes, because you are so close to the kerb after having completed the reverse, you have difficulty in turning left at the end of the road. You should have moved away from the kerb a little by the time you reach the end of the road to be in a better position to turn the corner.

Only practice will improve the reverse, so from now on at least one reverse should be attempted every lesson.

By the time you take the driving test, you must be able to do the reverse and the turn in the road without any difficulty. The important part of the test is the road procedure of normal driving, and it would be pointless to accomplish this and then to fail because of a bad reverse or turn in the road. Remember that you will be nervous on the test, so if there are any problems with these two manoeuvres, they will almost certainly let you down.

Some learners have more difficulty with the reverse than with the turn in the road. The reason is that judgement comes into a reverse more because every kerb is slightly different. It is helpful therefore if you practise the reverse manoeuvre on several different types of corners.

Reversing on a hill

It is a good idea to practise, in later lessons, a reverse either up or downhill. Do not choose a road with too steep a gradient at first; this can be attempted later when you have had more practice. It is possible that the examiner will choose a slight hill on the test for the reverse to be demonstrated so it is important that you are prepared.

Downhill

The only difference when reversing downhill is that the clutch and brake should be used instead of the clutch and accelerator. You should hold the car with the foot brake when the hand brake is released. Then, keeping the clutch depressed you should lift your foot from the brake and let the car roll back very slowly, being ready to apply the foot brake again if necessary. Apart from this the procedure is exactly the same.

Although it is wrong to allow the car to 'roll' or 'coast' in many circumstances it is permissible when manoeuvring at a very slow speed.

Uphill

When reversing uphill the procedure is exactly the same as for the normal reverse, except that the car will need more acceleration when moving off. It is possible for a reverse to be a combination of the above. In other words it could start by being an uphill reverse and then when the corner is turned, become a downhill reverse. It is just a case of practising as many different types of reverse as possible.

Reversing to the right

Although it is very rare for an examiner to ask a candidate on a test to do this, it could happen. It is therefore wise to practise it a few times.

It is of course, much easier to reverse round a righthand corner than a lefthand corner because the kerb can be seen all the way round. The same control of the car is needed but it is much easier to judge the distance from the kerb. The most difficult problem of the righthand reverse is positioning the car correctly to start.

The problem is that you have to move over to the 'wrong' side of the road. If you move over too early you will endanger traffic emerging from the side road.

The correct procedure is as follows:

1. The examiner will ask you to stop on the lefthand side of the road, some yards before the turning and then tell you to move into a position just past the turning on the right to reverse round the corner to the right.

2. After looking in the mirror and over the right shoulder and checking that no vehicle is going to emerge from the side road, you should give a right signal and move to the centre of the road as if you are going to turn into the side road.

3. When the centre of the road is reached and you are level with the centre of the side road you should, if it is safe, move across into a position some three to four metres (4–5 yards) past the turning, approximately 30 cm (12 in) from the kerb. From then on the procedure is the same as for the lefthand reverse except that you should look out of the righthand side of the car. It is a good idea to look out of the side window to check the distance from the kerb.

One final point:

Observation

As with the lefthand reverse observation is vitally important. You must look all round before moving off. You must glance out of the front before turning the corner.

You must watch for vehicles turning into the side road. You must watch out for pedestrians.

You have now been taught everything, apart from the emergency stop, that you need to know about the control of the car. You may feel that you are not very good at it yet, but having learned the basic principles properly, it will only need practice to improve. How much practice depends on the individual, but it is safe to say that the more you get the better. It is vital, though, that you do everything in the correct manner throughout all of the practice, otherwise you could develop bad habits. You should also by now have a basic knowledge of road procedure. The importance of good observation (mirror, looking over your shoulder and looking correctly at the end of the road), and correct positioning has been emphasised. It is now time for you to become acquainted with some of the hazards and problems of driving.

Because of the volume of traffic these days, it will take a considerable amount of time for any learner to gain the experience necessary to drive safely. The more practice you can get from now until your driving test, the better, and the more likely you are to pass.

I will no longer set the course out lesson by lesson. It will now be written as five lessons at a time, because the amount of knowledge to be taken in could not possibly be learnt in one lesson. I say five lessons for convenience sake. It could be more, depending on your ability. Some learners have great difficulty in passing this stage. Be patient, because you will find that once you have had enough practice, you will become a good driver.

You should study the notes on bends and junctions (pages 28–40) once again because now that you have had a little more practice at corners, you will be able to relate the knowledge that you have now gained to the notes.

Lessons Six to Ten – Preparation

Night driving

Although in the earlier lessons it is advisable to drive in the daylight, sometime or other you will need to practise at night. When
you do you will find that there are few extra problems to cope
with.

When you drive at night the most important thing is to be able to
see others and for others to be able to see you. You must, therefore,
be sure that your windscreen is clean and that your lights are *all*
working properly. Always drive with dipped headlights in built-up
areas, unless the road is well lit, but remember that when you park
the car they should be switched off, and do not park on the wrong
side of the road (the reflectors at the rear of the car should always
face oncoming traffic). There are certain places (e.g. in higher than
30 mph speed limits) where you should keep your parking lights on
and you should read your *Highway Code* for this further information on parking at night.

Do not necessarily wait until the official lighting up time to switch
your lights on because darkness can fall earlier, especially in the
winter and even when dusk, especially if you are driving a dark
coloured car, it is difficult for other people to see you.

When you first drive at night you will probably want to drive more
slowly because you will find that the headlights from other cars will
make it more difficult for you to see. You will soon get used to the
other vehicle's lights but even when you do it is important that you
give yourself more time to slow down or stop, so keep further back
when following other vehicles. Slow down that extra bit more when

approaching any hazards. Be especially careful at pedestrian crossings, traffic lights and anywhere pedestrians could be because at night the shadows can hide the dangers from you until it is too late.

It is more difficult to judge the speed of other vehicles in darkness so be extra careful when emerging at junctions. Use your ears as well as your eyes at all times. Try not to inconvenience other people by dazzling them with your headlights, especially when following another car, so stay further back.

If you are dazzled by somebody else's headlights, then you should slow down, or even stop if necessary.

Be especially careful when overtaking at night because it is more difficult to see the road ahead and to judge distances. The flashing of your lights is better than the use of the horn for warning others of your presence at night and remember that between the hours of 11.30 p.m. and 7.00 a.m. it is illegal to sound the horn.

Bad weather conditions

Rain

You may have already experienced driving in the rain on one of the lessons; if you have not you no doubt soon will. It takes a bit of getting used to because with the windscreen wipers going and the swish of the tyres on the road it is more difficult to hear the sound of the engine. Visibility is also often restricted so be sure that others can see you by using the dipped headlights. Leave more time to slow down and stop by keeping further back from other vehicles because any harsh braking or sudden turning of the wheel could cause you to skid. Also be alert for pedestrians while driving at night, especially in shopping areas, near crossings, junctions and traffic lights. Drive slowly, look further ahead of you and try to anticipate the actions of others as early as possible to give yourself a chance to act correctly. It takes about twice the road distance to stop a car (see page 101) on a wet road, so you must be ready for any emergency.

One other problem which affects all drivers when it is raining is the misting up of windows and mirrors. These days, most cars are fitted with demisters but you can help the visibility by keeping windows partly open so that the air circulates.

Ice and snow

While you are learning you should not attempt to drive on icy roads because, with your inexperience, it will be a danger to yourself and other people. You must, however, become familiar with driving in such conditions, therefore when you have passed the driving test you should, when the opportunity arises, gain some experience on icy or snow-covered roads.

Before you start driving, make sure that any ice or snow is cleared from all of the windows and outside mirrors of the vehicle. If there is any risk of ice on the road you must drive slowly and approach bends or junctions with extreme caution. Any harsh braking or sudden turning of the wheel must be avoided otherwise you could lose control of the vehicle by going into a skid. All of the problems that were discussed in the previous paragraph about wet conditions apply in icy conditions and skidding will be discussed a little later.

Fog

As in snow and ice, it is better not to drive when it is very foggy while you are inexperienced. Of course, there are different degrees of fog, so you will have to decide with your instructor whether the conditions are good enough for you to have a lesson.

Once again, if you drive in fog you must travel more slowly than normal and keep a further distance from the vehicle in front. Always have dipped headlights on because other people must be able to see you. Sidelights are useless in foggy conditions, because it is usual to see the car even before its sidelights – which defeats the purpose of having them on. Full beam may reflect back into your own eyes, making it difficult for you to see. At junctions and roundabouts, use your ears as well as your eyes, to warn you of other vehicles approaching. One of the greatest dangers in fog is the driver who thinks that he knows the road and therefore drives too fast in the mistaken belief that all is safe. It is impossible to know the road in fog, however many times you have been along it; you may know where it leads, but you do not know what hidden dangers there are.

Never park the car on the road during foggy conditions if you can avoid it. If it is essential, however, make sure that you leave the lights on and you park on the correct side of the road.

Skidding

The most important lesson to learn about skidding is that you should do your utmost not to get into a skid in the first place. Any driver can get out of a skid safely given a small amount of skill and knowhow, a lot of time and an enormous amount of luck! The trouble is that by the time the driver has managed to stop the car skidding, he has probably hit something or somebody. It is one thing to practise skidding control on a specially built skid pan, but entirely another proposition when you are on the road and restricted for space and time.

How do you avoid getting into a skid?

First you must know the causes of skidding. We mentioned, when talking about icy conditions, that harsh braking, harsh acceleration, excessive speed on a bend or sudden turning of the wheels can cause the car to skid. It does not have to be icy for the car to skid because even in dry conditions the road could be covered in oil and the surface therefore slippery, but it is not the road surface that causes the skid, it is the driver.

No car would skid unless the driver caused it to do so, even in the worst icy conditions. By correct handling of the car skidding can be avoided by:

1. Looking out for possible slippery surfaces. This could be muddy, oily, greasy, wet or icy roads.
2. Looking out for road signs warning you of slippery conditions.
3. Driving more slowly when there is a possibility of skidding.
4. Keeping further back from other moving vehicles in bad weather.
5. Braking gently and in good time when approaching bends and hazards.
6. Steering evenly and gently on bends and corners.
7. Accelerating gently when moving away or increasing speed.
8. Keeping your tyres in good condition and at the correct pressure.
9. Anticipating any possible dangers well in advance, thereby giving yourself more time.

Any sudden movement, then, can cause the car to skid and on certain road surfaces and in certain conditions skidding is more likely.

How to control a skid
If you do skid, and as nobody is perfect it is quite possible that one day you might, you must have some idea as to how to control the car. What you do to deal with the skid depends on what caused the skid in the first place.

Immediate action
Foot off the brake and/or accelerator, then corrective action according to whether the rear, front or all four wheels are skidding.

1. Skid caused by braking too hard.
    If you were driving in a straight line, you would probably skid in a straight line. As the act of braking has caused the skid, then your first action must be to release the brake. Once having released the brake you can apply the brake again but more gently this time. If you then skid again, keep taking your foot off the brake and on it again until you stop. It is no good keeping your foot on the brake because you will keep skidding in a straight line.
2. Skid caused by steering too harshly.
    Take your foot off the accelerator or brake, whichever it happened to be on at the time of the skid, and steer the car in the same direction as the skid. This means if the back of the car skids to the left then turn the wheel to the left or vice versa.
3. Skid caused by accelerating too fiercely.
    Ease your foot off the accelerator and turn the wheel if necessary, as above.

Tyres

The tyres are the only contact you have with the road, so you must be certain that they are in good condition. It is not sufficient to be just within the limits of the law because unless you have good treads and the tyre walls are free of cuts and bulges, you are flirting with danger.

The correct pressure of air in your tyres must be adhered to. It is vital to check the pressure at least every week with a proper gauge because it is impossible to judge the pressure just by looking at the tyre. The handbook for the car will give you the details of correct tyre pressure.

Most tyres these days are radials but if you have to buy a new tyre, make sure that it is the correct type. It can be dangerous to fit a crossply tyre if the other tyres on the car are radials. Consult your local tyre dealer for advice on this subject, but very briefly the tyre fittings that should be followed are:

1.	Radial tyres on all four wheels	SAFE
2.	Crossply tyres on all four wheels	SAFE
3.	Radial tyres on rear axle with crossply tyres on front axle	SAFE
4.	All other combinations	UNSAFE

Try not to touch the kerb when driving. This can easily happen when you are parking so be careful because it can cause considerable damage to the tyre. Apart from being expensive, it can be dangerous because it may have weakened the wall of the tyre so much that it causes a blow-out. Try also to avoid large bumps in the road as this will cause damage to the tyre.

Blow-outs

This is the term used when the tyre bursts. Although it is very rare these days it can be dangerous because the steering is immediately affected, possibly causing the car to suddenly swerve. You can see the importance of always driving with both hands on the wheel, because if a 'blow-out' occurs when you have only one hand on the wheel it will be difficult to control the car. When the tyre bursts, hold tightly on to the steering wheel to check the swerving and brake gently. Heavy braking would cause the swerving to increase.

Aqua-planing

This is the name given to the unusual occurrence of the tyres losing their grip on the road in very heavy rain and floods. At speed the car will run on a cushion of water which will greatly hamper the control of the car. To avoid this happening make sure that you see where the road is flooded and slow down accordingly. If the car starts to aqua-plane treat it the same way as if you are on ice (i.e. no harsh braking or sudden steering).

When driving at night in the earlier lessons your instructor will be controlling the lights because you will have enough to worry about without concerning yourself with dipping headlights. Later it will be possible for you to control the lights yourself with your instructor's guidance.

Before having a lesson in the rain you should know how to switch on the windscreen wipers but do not worry about such things as working the demister and heater until you are much more advanced. Leave this to your instructor at first.

In really bad conditions such as thick fog or snow, it is better not to go out at all. It is far too dangerous and of very little help to the inexperienced learner. After you have passed the test is the time to practise in these conditions.

Lessons Six to Ten – Practice

Duration of each lesson one hour

You should plan your routes for these lessons to include as many hazards and problems as possible, preferably gradually increasing the number of difficult situations in each lesson. Try to find different routes so that you get experience on as many different roads as possible.

One hour at a time is still sufficient, because you will still be concentrating hard every lesson.

You can start the lesson from anywhere you like provided that you don't take yourself into a very difficult situation within the first 100 metres (yards) or so. Remember you still need time to get used to the car, and for your initial nerves to go when you first start to drive at the beginning of every lesson.

Every lesson should, if possible, include all that has been taught in the previous lessons, i.e. hill starts, left turns, right turns, turning in the road, reverse, etc. If you are having difficulty with any particular manoeuvre, then spend a little extra time on it.

You may have forgotten or become confused about something that was taught in one of the very early lessons. Do not worry. Just get your instructor to explain it to you and then practise it. (I have known learners to have had about 15 lessons and then suddenly to have forgotten that the clutch must be depressed when stopping.) Although your instructor should still be talking you through everything, gradually you will find that you are doing things as he says them.

Always give clear direction instructions early. If there is any possibility that he mis-heard you or he does the wrong thing, repeat your instruction. Be ready for anything! At least half of each lesson should be on side roads, and the other half on busier roads.

There follow explanations and diagrams on the various hazards that will be encountered on these lessons.

Explain these to him before the lessons, and when any of the hazards are experienced on the lessons, it is a good idea to stop in a convenient place and explain the hazard.

Pedestrian crossings

A.   Uncontrolled pedestrian crossings (zebra crossings)

The law is that a pedestrian always has the right of way on a zebra crossing. This means that once a pedestrian has stepped on to a crossing you must stop. Always look well ahead for pedestrian crossings, so as to give yourself plenty of time to stop if necessary.

They are well marked with flashing yellow beacons (Belisha Beacons), black and white stripes and zig zag white lines on both sides, so there is no excuse for not seeing a crossing well in advance.

There are two different types of zebra crossings:

1.   Uncontrolled pedestrian crossings going across the full width of the road. (See Fig. 24.)

   At these crossings you must give way to a pedestrian even if he has stepped on to the crossing from the other side of the road, and you must not proceed until the crossing is completely clear.

   You should wait until the pedestrian has walked *completely off the crossing*, even if he is walking away from you to the other side of the road. Until he has walked off the crossing, the crossing is closed to traffic.

   The reason for this is that while he is still on the crossing, it is possible for another pedestrian to step or even run out on to it, and you must wait for him too.

2.   Uncontrolled pedestrian crossings with an island in the middle. (See Fig. 25.)

   This type of crossing is treated as two separate crossings, the island being the centre with a crossing on each side. You only have to stop if somebody is on your side of the island. However,

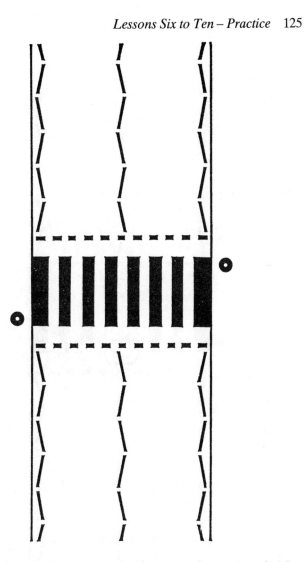

Fig. 24 A zebra crossing – one crossing (you must give way to pedestrians anywhere on the crossing).

if somebody is walking towards your side of the crossing, but has not reached the island, it is better to stop, because they are obviously going to want to cross your side as well.

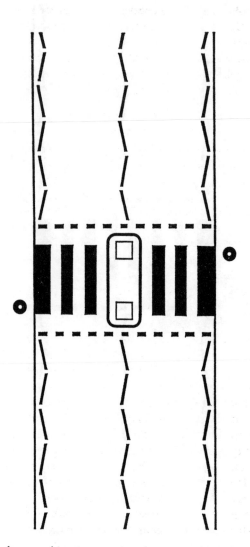

Fig. 25   A zebra crossing – two crossings (you must give way to pedestrians on the crossing on your side of the road).

B. Controlled pedestrian crossings (pelican crossings)
These are the crossings with traffic lights controlling them, often called 'pelican' crossings.

You must stop when the lights are showing amber or red. When the flashing amber lights appear, you may proceed so long as nobody is still crossing the road.

General comments regarding pedestrian crossings
1. Always approach all types of pedestrian crossings with caution. They are usually in busy areas, so there is always the likelihood of somebody suddenly deciding to cross the road.
   You must be ready to stop!
2. Your view of the crossing is sometimes restricted as you approach, so slow down sufficiently and be ready.
3. Always be ready for the car in front of you to stop suddenly as you approach the crossing.
4. Try not to stop suddenly yourself at a crossing (remember the car behind you). You must look in your mirror and, if necessary, give a slowing down signal (right arm out of the window and moved up and down) to warn those following and to inform pedestrians.
5. Never give dangerous signals to pedestrians. In other words, do not wave a pedestrian across the road, even if there is some hesitation. It is up to the pedestrian to decide whether it is safe to cross or not. (The reason for this is that if you wave a pedestrian across, he may take your signal for granted and not bother to check that it is safe. This could result in his being run down by another vehicle.) You should, however, give the stopping signal with your arm as you approach the crossing to inform the pedestrian who is about to cross that you intend to stop. It is, therefore, important to have your window open if there is any possibility of an arm signal being needed.
6. If you are in a traffic queue, always make sure that you leave pedestrian crossings clear. Do not stop on a crossing.

You should always stop at a crossing if there is the slightest possibility of someone stepping on to the crossing. Hesitation is fatal, because if you slow down as though you are going to stop, but then continue on, it causes confusion with the pedestrian, who might step on to the crossing, with terrible consequences.

Pedestrians at junctions

You must give way to pedestrians who are crossing the road into which you are turning. Always be ready to do this.

Pedestrian crossings always cause trouble to the inexperienced driver. He will tend not to notice them, so always be looking out for them yourself and warn him if he appears to be approaching one too fast.

Subconsciously, he will not want to stop at a crossing because of the problems of moving away again in busy traffic. You must encourage him to stop, and let him take his time in moving away at first until he gains confidence. Always be ready to take action at pedestrian crossings. The pupil may put his foot on the wrong pedal.

Zig-zag lines

These lines are some 25 metres (26 yards) or so on both sides of the crossing. They warn of the approach of a crossing. You must not stop in the area of these lines except to give people precedence at the crossing. You must not overtake the moving motor vehicle nearest the crossing, or the leading vehicle which has stopped to give way to a pedestrian on the crossing.

Box junctions   (See Fig. 26)

These are found at busy junctions, usually traffic lights, and the idea of them is to keep the traffic flowing. They are marked with criss-cross yellow lines in the middle of the junction. You must not enter these lines unless your exit is clear. In other words, you must not stop on the lines.

The only exception is when turning right and your way is only blocked by oncoming traffic. You may then wait in the normal place in the centre of the road until it is safe for you to turn.

Of course the marking of box junctions would not be necessary if drivers used their common sense. You should never enter any junction if you would block it by doing so.

Dual carriageways

There is usually a higher speed limit on dual carriageways and therefore the general speed of traffic is higher. Because of this it is

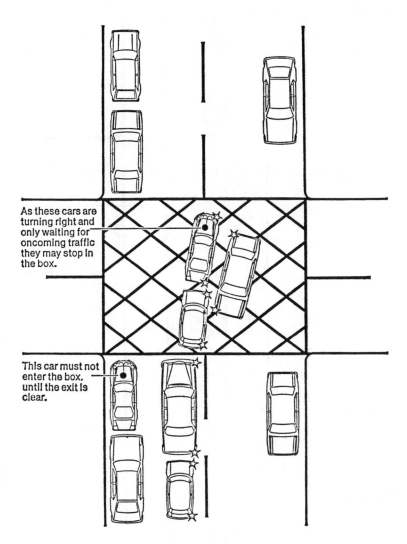

As these cars are turning right and only waiting for oncoming traffic they may stop in the box.

This car must not enter the box until the exit is clear.

Fig. 26 A box junction.

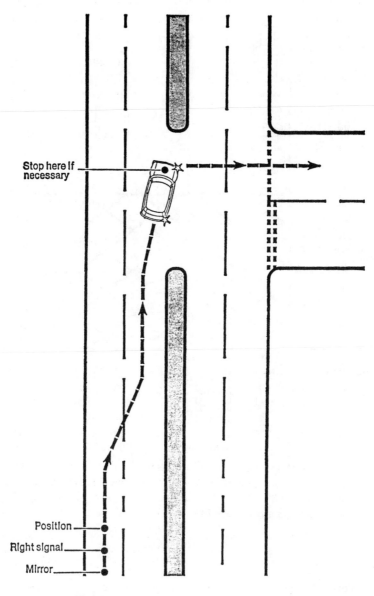

Fig. 27 Turning right off a dual carriageway.

important that any manoeuvre should be started very early to allow enough time to complete the manoeuvre safely.

Turning right off a dual carriageway (See Fig. 27)

This manoeuvre is probably the most difficult and can often cause problems to the inexperienced.

Presume you are travelling down the left lane of a dual carriageway when the instruction is given to turn right at the next road or roundabout.

(You must give the instruction to turn right very early.)

After having looked in your mirror and given your signal you must keep up with the speed of the other traffic. As soon as possible you have to move over to the righthand lane, but if your speed drops so that you are travelling more slowly than the traffic that is already in the righthand lane, you will find it impossible to move across.

The procedure is as follows:

1. Look in mirror (without slowing down).
2. Signal right, even if it is not immediately safe to move over to the righthand lane, because this will give early warning to following traffic of your intention to turn right.

   Provided that you are keeping up with the flow of traffic you will soon find a space to move over to the right, but make quite sure that it is safe to do so.

   A quick glance over your right shoulder is advisable.
3. Move over to the righthand lane if safe to do so.
4. Start slowing down on the brake and change down gears as you would for any other right turn.
5. When the central reservation is reached, stop in as safe a position as possible until the other carriageway is clear for you to make the turn. The same procedure applies if you are approaching a roundabout on a dual carriageway.

The earlier the pupil is instructed to turn right the better. He must be given time to move across. Be sure that *you* look round before he changes lanes, because he will find it difficult to judge the speed of the following traffic.

You will probably have to tell him when to move across at first, but with practice, his judgement will improve.

Turning right on to a dual carriageway   (See Fig. 28)
The important thing when turning right on to a dual carriageway
is to keep in the correct position when you reach the central
reservation.

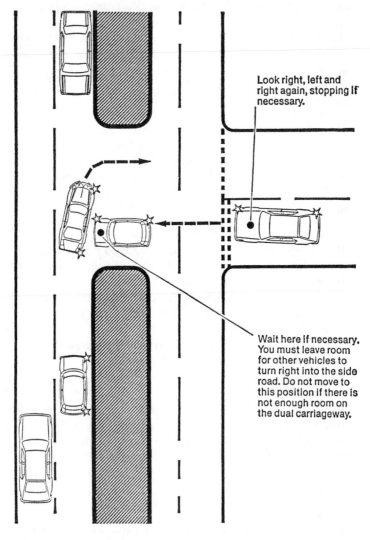

Look right, left and
right again, stopping if
necessary.

Wait here if necessary.
You must leave room
for other vehicles to
turn right into the side
road. Do not move to
this position if there is
not enough room on
the dual carriageway.

Fig. 28   Turning right on to a dual carriageway.

Dual carriageways are treated as two separate roads. You must wait until the carriageway nearest you is safe to cross, then move to the centre reservation. When the other carriageway is clear you may then proceed. When you reach the centre reservation you must keep to the left to allow other vehicles to turn right into the road you have come from.

If the central reservation is not wide enough for you to wait safely in without endangering other vehicles on the dual carriageway, then the manoeuvre must be completed in one movement (i.e. as for entering from any other junction).

Procedure for the manoeuvre is as follows:

1. Stop (if necessary) at the end of the road.
2. Look RIGHT, LEFT and RIGHT AGAIN.
3. If the first carriageway is clear, move to the centre reservation.
4. Stop (if necessary), in a safe position well to the left.
5. Look LEFT, RIGHT and LEFT AGAIN (traffic coming from the left).
6. If safe, continue.

If there is a car in front of you also turning right, and it is already in the central reservation, it is better to wait for it to go before you proceed to the centre.

Never get stuck in the carriageway.

Remember it is difficult to judge the speed of a car when it is travelling towards you, so give yourself plenty of time to move across the carriageway.

Traffic tends to be very fast on a dual carriageway.

While waiting at any busy road junction it is very important to be ready to move off when the opportunity comes, so always be in gear with some acceleration.

When it is safe you can then move by just lifting the clutch (and releasing the hand brake if it is on).

Sometimes you have to wait a long time at these busy roads and if you miss your opportunity to go, you could be there for ever.

Be sure it is safe.

Turning left on to a dual carriageway
It is the same as any other left turn, but make sure that you look RIGHT, LEFT and RIGHT AGAIN.

It is often thought that it is only necessary to look right because the traffic is only coming from the right. But remember, you are looking left not only for vehicles, but also for pedestrians who could be crossing the road. There could also be somebody reversing, or for that matter somebody could be driving the wrong way down the carriageway. It does happen!

So ALWAYS look RIGHT, LEFT and RIGHT AGAIN.

Try to gain as much practice as possible on dual carriageways. You could be taken on one in your test, but apart from that, it is essential for your future driving once you have passed your test.

One-way streets and systems

It is vital that you know you are approaching a one-way system or that you are on a one-way street. There are always plenty of signs to warn you, but you must be looking out for them.

Once on a one-way road the golden rule is to stay in one lane and not to keep swapping from one lane to the next, especially when negotiating a bend.

Usually you should keep to the left lane unless you are turning right, or if sign posts or road markings dictate otherwise. If you are going to turn right then get into the right lane as early and safely as possible.

If you have to change lanes, do so by using your mirror and signalling early as on a dual carriageway.

When going straight on be guided by the road markings. If there is not enough room for a middle lane of traffic you will have to choose either the right or left lane, choose early and stay in that lane.

Remember traffic often travels faster on a one-way system, so be extra sure that it is safe.

Also remember that other vehicles are allowed to overtake you on your LEFT so watch out for them.

Never hesitate once you have decided that it is safe to proceed.

Always be sure that you know where you are going in good time, otherwise there will be confusion.

Turning right off a one-way road   (See Fig. 29)
This is similar to turning right off a dual carriageway. You must get over to the right as early as possible. If you are turning

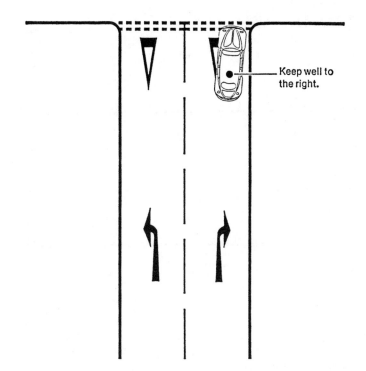

Keep well to the right.

Fig. 29   A one-way road – turning right.

right at the end of the road, you must be as far to the right as possible.

The examiner in your test will not tell you that you are on a one-way system, so it is up to you to see the signs.

Practise with your pupil in some one-way streets. Always give clear directions very early. It is quite in order to instruct the pupil to follow the directional road markings to wherever you are headed, provided that such directional road markings are clear. It is a good idea to drive round the one-way system yourself to get the feel of it before you take the pupil on it.

If there is hesitation in the pupil's driving on these types of road, then further practice is essential, but do not overdo it.

It is sometimes better to leave it until the next lesson if harassment is felt.

(a) 3-lane road

(b) 4-lane road

(c) Dual carriageway

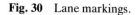

Fig. 30 Lane markings.

Road markings

These days the roads are full of white and yellow lines which can be very confusing to an inexperienced driver. For this moment we will ignore the yellow lines and concentrate on the white.

These white lines break down into three categories. They are (1) information lines, (2) warning lines, (3) mandatory lines.

1.   Information lines
These are mainly lane markings (see Fig. 30) or direction arrows (see Fig. 31).

Lane markings   (See Fig. 30)
These broken lines are just dividing the road into equal widths or lanes. You should normally keep to the lefthand lane unless you are overtaking, turning right or avoiding an obstruction.
  NEVER WANDER FROM LANE TO LANE.

Direction arrows   (See Fig. 31)
Always look well ahead for the direction arrows and keep in the correct lane as early as possible.

2.   Warning lines
Centre line
The white line down the centre of the road has two purposes. One is to mark the centre of the road and the other is to warn of approaching hazards. As the spaces between the lines become shorter and the lines longer, you are approaching a hazard.

  The hazard could be a keep left sign (see Fig. 32a), traffic lights, junction, bend (see Fig. 32b), etc. As the lines become longer, you must be more careful. Although they are only warning lines it would be dangerous to cross the lines as they lengthen.

3.   Mandatory lines
Double white lines   (See Fig. 33)
These are down the centre of the road and if the continuous white line is nearest you then YOU MUST NOT cross it. If the broken line is nearest to you, then you can only cross it if it is safe to do so.

Lines approaching junctions   (See Fig. 34) [Hatched markings]
These are really lane markings with some lanes blocked out by

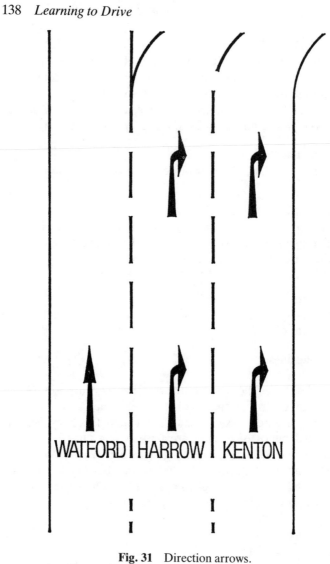

Fig. 31 Direction arrows.

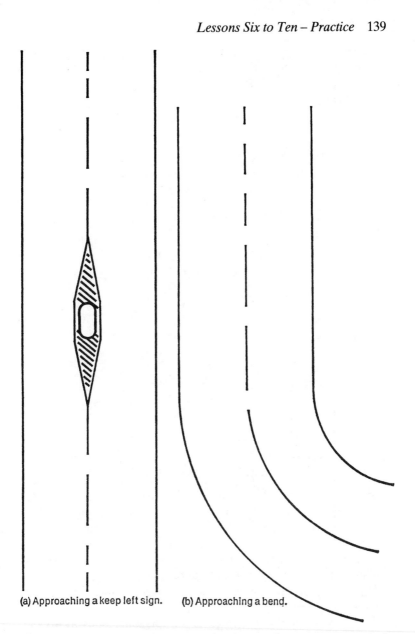

(a) Approaching a keep left sign.   (b) Approaching a bend.

Fig. 32   Centre line markings – these lines become longer as you approach a hazard.

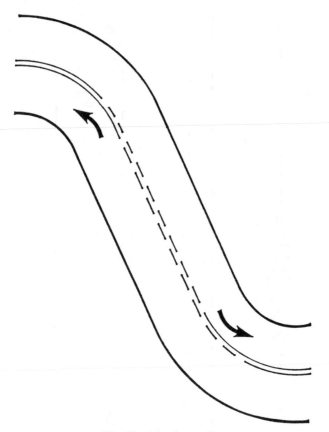

Fig. 33   Mandatory lines.

criss-cross markings. They are usually at dangerous junctions on busy roads. They are both warning and mandatory depending upon which direction you are coming from and where you are intending to go.

The golden rule is not to enter the diagonal striped lines if you are going to continue straight on without turning.

If you are turning, then only enter the diagonal lines if it is safe to do so.

It would be better not to enter the diagonal lines at all but sometimes this is unavoidable when turning right, especially on very fast roads.

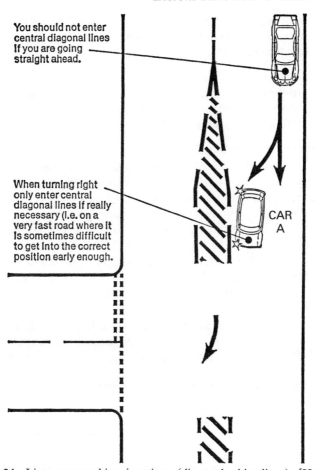

You should not enter central diagonal lines if you are going straight ahead.

When turning right only enter central diagonal lines if really necessary (i.e. on a very fast road where it is sometimes difficult to get into the correct position early enough.

CAR A

Fig. 34 Lines approaching junctions (diagonal white lines). [Hatched markings].

The diagram in Fig. 34 illustrates this. In this diagram Car A is travelling at a speed of 50 mph to keep up with the flow of the other traffic.

It would be necessary for him to slow down considerably before he entered the gap where the arrow is, thereby endangering traffic behind him, or he would have to enter the space much too quickly.

It is better for Car A to move over slightly earlier even if it means entering the diagonal lines for a short distance.

There should be no danger in this because the vehicles travelling in the opposite direction should not go into the centre lane if they are going straight on. They must keep to the left.

Stop Lines   (See Fig. 35)
These are the double continuous white lines at the end of the road where you must stop. They are accompanied by a circular stop sign or the new red octagonal stop sign.

Give way lines   (See Fig. 36)
These are double broken white lines at the end of the road. They mean that you must give way to traffic on the main road. They are often accompanied by a triangular GIVE WAY sign, and there is an inverted triangle painted in the road as you approach the lines.

Remember that you do not have to stop at these lines, but you must look RIGHT, LEFT and RIGHT AGAIN before emerging into the road, and you must be travelling slowly enough to stop.

At some junctions there appear to be two sets of white lines. One line shows the continuation of the road, the other lines are normal give way lines.

There is a single broken white line at roundabouts to denote the give way point and there is a single continuous white line at traffic lights behind which you must stop when the lights turn to amber.

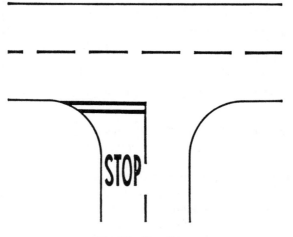

Fig. 35   Stop lines.

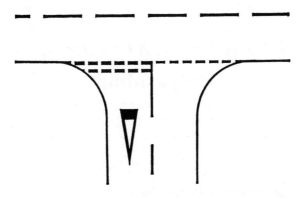

Fig. 36   Give way lines.

At some junctions, mainly at traffic lights, the procedure when turning right is altered; there are arrows to show this. (See Fig. 13.)

Yellow lines
These are parking restrictions and are explained fully in the *Highway Code*. We will be dealing with more hazards in the next section.

Lessons Eleven to Fifteen – Preparation

Applying for the driving test

It is now time that you applied for a driving test appointment. There is usually a two- to three-month delay from the time that the test is applied for to the date of the actual test and sometimes the delay can be as long as six months. It is better, therefore, to apply for the test at an early stage rather than wait until you are up to the required standard, and then have to wait another three months.

You can obtain an application for the driving test form from the Post Office. This should be completed by you, with your instructor's help if necessary, and then sent to the address stated on the form accompanied with the correct fee. Where the form asks for the 'earliest date' you should put the date at which the instructor thinks you will be ready for the test. He will have to advise you on this point because it depends upon your progress. If you leave a two- to three-month gap between the present date and the date of the test, it will probably be about right. If you do not make the progress hoped for in that time the test can be postponed, provided that three clear days' notice is given. Remember though that the three days' notice does not include weekends or Bank Holidays so when you receive your appointment card for the test, check the final day of cancellation which will be noted on the card.

After having sent your application form to the Traffic Area Office it usually takes about two weeks for the appointment card to arrive. If there is a delay of over three weeks and there is still no sign of the appointment card the Traffic Area Office should be contacted.

Lessons Eleven to Fifteen – Practice

During the previous lessons you have been practising on all types of roads and should by now be acquainted with at least some of the hazards and problems of driving.

You have been relying on your instructor for advice and encouragement. He has been warning you of possible dangerous situations and helping you when you have got into difficulties. This is how it should be, because up to now you have had so many other things to concentrate on (such as controlling the car), that to try to have enough concentration on the road would be impossible.

At this stage, however, you must start to think for yourself. Now, of course, you cannot suddenly expect to do everything on your own straight away. It will be a gradual transition between your instructor talking through each procedure as it occurs to your eventually doing everything without being told.

Instead of telling him what to do each time, let him do it himself a few times. This especially applies to gear changing and slowing down. Remind him to change gear or slow down if you think he has left it too late, and of course do not let him get into difficulties which could be dangerous.

One of the most difficult problems for the inexperienced is to be able to anticipate danger. You will find that time and again you will drive into dangerous situations which would be obvious to an experienced driver, but which you do not even notice. Practice will help, but only if you know the dangers that you are looking for.

There follow some helpful points that will be of use to both you and your instructor. Read these with him and ask him to explain anything that you do not understand.

Anticipation

Remember that even though you are a learner, the traffic conditions and hazards are the same for you as they are for the experienced driver. You both use the same roads!

Until now your experience has come from your instructor, but from now on you must start thinking and acting for yourself. This will not come easily, but with effort and practice it will not be too long before you feel that you are not only in full control of the car, but also of all the problems of driving.

You must be able to anticipate.

This does not mean that you anticipate what is going to happen, but what could happen.

Remember, never presume anything. There are numerous possibilities for any situation.

To illustrate this, I will ask a question that your examiner could ask you in your driving test:

Q.   The right indicator of the car in front of you is flashing. What information does this give you?

A.   That the electrics in his car are functioning.

That is all you can be certain about. The fact that his indicator is flashing could mean many things:

1.   He is turning right at the next road.
2.   He is turning right at the second road.
3.   He is turning right somewhere.
4.   He is turning into a driveway on the right.
5.   He is stopping on the righthand side of the road.
6.   He is going to do a 'U' turn.
7.   He is turning left. (People do put the wrong indicator on sometimes.)
8.   He is not turning at all. (He could have put it on by mistake, or have forgotten to cancel it after taking his last turning.)

I have listed eight possibilities, and there are probably more that you can think of.

You can see from any one situation the possibilities are endless. There follow several examples which should help you to think more when driving.

Traffic lights

1. When approaching traffic lights, never presume that they will stay on one colour. In fact always expect them to change.

    If they are green as you approach always slow down enough to be able to stop safely. (Remember you must stop at an amber light.) It will be necessary to change down gear as well as braking. 3rd gear is often sufficient, depending upon traffic conditions.
2. Never presume that because the lights are green in your favour that nobody will pull across you at the junction; cars do not always stop at red lights. They should, but sometimes they don't!

    Also remember that pedestrians often become confused at traffic lights, especially when there is a filter.
3. When pulling away from a stationary position at traffic lights, never presume:

    (*a*) That the road in front has cleared.
    (*b*) That the car in front of you will move off straight away. (Even experienced drivers stall their engines!)

Road junctions and crossroads

Just because there are double white lines and give way or stop signs at junctions, never presume that other cars are going to stop at them. Remember there is no barrier at the end of the road, so if the driver of the other vehicle is not thinking, it is quite possible for him to come straight across the road in front of you.

You are especially vulnerable at crossroads. You only have to notice the amount of broken glass at crossroads to realise the number of times that accidents happen there. Crossroads have been covered earlier in the course, so it is sufficient to say that whatever type of road you are on, always be prepared for the worst to happen at these junctions.

Other vehicles

A. Cars

1. Remember that when somebody is signalling to turn, there are several possibilities:

(*a*) You are not sure WHERE he is turning.
(*b*) You are not sure IF he is turning.
(*c*) You are not sure what position the other car will get into.
(*d*) He might change his mind.

2. When following a line of cars look well ahead. See any possible danger early and be ready to act. Looking only at the car in front could mean that you are much too late to act.

3. Use your common sense with other people's driving. If an elderly person is driving, remember that their reaction might be slow. If someone is driving with young children or an animal in the car, his attention could suddenly be distracted.

Remember:
(*a*) If somebody looks inexperienced, he probably is.
(*b*) If somebody looks drunk he probably is.
(*c*) If somebody looks to be a good driver, do not presume that he is. Anybody can make a mistake – even good drivers!

B.   Buses
Buses always create problems for learners.

Remember:
1. Buses stop at bus stops. Look for people on the platform of the bus as this is a good guide that a bus stop is coming up.

2. Buses often stop in awkward positions so do not presume that you will be able to pass it as soon as it stops. This is especially important with the very long single decker buses.

3. Buses very often pull out quickly from bus stops. One of the unfortunate problems of driving is that the larger the vehicle, the more likely it is going to pull out in front of you.

The same applies when meeting other vehicles through narrow gaps. Never presume that the other vehicle is going to stop for you. They rarely do.

4. When stopping behind a bus at a bus stop, keep well back so that you can see round the bus. You do not know for how long the bus will be stationary so you may have to overtake it. If you are too close behind it this will be impossible.

C.   Large vehicles
When you are following a large slow-moving vehicle, always stay

further back than you would behind a smaller vehicle. This is because your vision is obscured by the larger vehicle. The further back you are the more you can see ahead of it.

Try to anticipate what a lorry is going to do, especially when it is turning left, parking or entering compounds. Very often, before turning left, he has to pull out to the right to enable him to negotiate the corner.

If a large vehicle is manoeuvring, never get too close and always wait until the manoeuvre has been completed. Stay well back!

D.   Milk Floats
These, like buses, cause great problems to the learner. Because of their very slow speed it is advisable to overtake them as soon as possible. This must, of course, be done safely. Do not follow too closely.

Milkmen tend to think more about their next deliveries than what is coming behind. Always be prepared for a milk float to stop, turn or pull out without warning.

E.   Stationary vehicles
They do not remain stationary for ever!

Always look to see if there is anybody in the driving seat of a stationary vehicle, especially when it appears to be parked near a junction or traffic lights. It is very easy to stop behind a parked vehicle thinking that it is about to move off, only to find that there is no driver.

If a lorry is parked near a junction, it is not so easy because you cannot see the driver, but you can see if the back of the lorry is open for unloading. Beware of parked vehicles suddenly moving off. Not everybody looks in their mirror and over their shoulder.

People open doors and pedestrians walk out in front of stationary vehicles, so give yourself plenty of room when passing.

F.   Vehicles reversing
Watch out for this because it is sometimes difficult to distinguish between a car that is stationary and one that is reversing.

It is also very difficult to detect which way a vehicle is going to turn when reversing, especially if they are trying to park.

Always keep well back and let them finish their manoeuvre before attempting to continue.

Remember that the front of a vehicle swings out to the right if they are reversing to the left.

Parking

When travelling through a busy shopping centre, motorists are often trying to park, and unfortunately thinking more about this than who is following. If you see somebody going very slowly in front of you, looking for a parking space, stay well back and be ready for him to stop suddenly.

Cyclists

A great danger on the road, and very difficult to anticipate. Many cyclists are children, who are very inexperienced on the road, so anything could happen.

Always leave plenty of room (at least six feet) when overtaking a cyclist.

Pedestrians

Pedestrians often do not realise the dangers on the road, especially the elderly or the very young.

Traffic lights and pedestrian crossings sometimes confuse them, and therefore take extreme care when there are pedestrians about. Pedestrians ALWAYS have the right of way if they are in the road. Remember that it is not just a scratch on your car but a life that is at stake. The responsibility is always with the driver.

Children

Children have no idea of the dangers of the road, so if you see a child on the pavement always be careful.

It is impossible to anticipate what a child is going to do, so you must be ready for anything.

If you see a child anywhere near the road you must slow down.

Animals

Dogs and cats can cause accidents so always beware.

If you see an animal anywhere near the road, drive with extreme caution because they can suddenly dart out in front of you, or another car, causing a swerve.

Equestrians

Horses are sometimes nervous and very unpredictable. Never sound your horn when approaching or about to overtake as this could obviously startle a horse and even cause him to bolt. Always approach very slowly and leave plenty of room when overtaking (a horse sideways on must be at least six feet wide!).

General

There is one thing all the above problems have in common. At all times you must be looking as far ahead and in as wide an arc as possible so that you are ready for any possibility. Obviously with more experience it will become easier to anticipate, but you must always be thinking about possible dangers.

Always cover the brake and be ready to slow down if there is any possibility of danger. Most accidents could be avoided if only the driver had been anticipating. It is impossible to say that it was all the other person's fault, because there was probably something that you could have done about it.

It will take time for the pupil to be good at anticipating, but you must tell him if you think that he has not seen danger or not acted early enough.

The biggest problem with regard to anticipation is often with pedestrians. For some reason or other, learners do not bother about pedestrians. Often they go within centimetres of a pedestrian or even drive straight for them.

You must realise the dangers and consequences of going too close to pedestrians.

I have had to stop the learner on several occasions to avoid hitting a pedestrian who has been crossing a junction when the traffic lights were green. When I asked why the pupil did not stop, the answer has been that the lights were in our favour so we had the right of way. It has then taken some time to convince the pupil of what might have happened if I had not stopped the car.

The only possible explanation for this, apart from homicidal tendencies, is that the pupil gets into the back of his mind that the road is only for vehicles, and that pedestrians should never be on the road.

You must dispel this notion and convince yourself that pedestrians ALWAYS HAVE THE RIGHT OF WAY.

Lessons Sixteen to Twenty – Preparation

Test appointment card

When the appointment card is received you should read it carefully to check:

1. That the date and time are convenient to you and the person who is going to accompany you.
2. The location of the Test Centre. It could be different from the one that was asked for.
3. The latest date for cancelling the test. This date is in the box at the bottom lefthand corner of the appointment card. If you have been given a date at very short notice you will find that instead of a date there will be a number of crosses in the box. In these circumstances you will not lose the fee if you cannot take the test. The Department of Transport will send another appointment in due course.

If there is any problem concerning the appointment you should telephone the Traffic Area Office on the number quoted on the back of the card. Never ring the Driving Test Centre (the number of which is on the front of the card) except in the case of fog, snow or ice on the day of the test.

The other information on the appointment card concerning items required (i.e. insurance, driving licence, etc.) should be studied to enable you to be ready for the test when the time comes. This is also a good time to check that the seat belts are in good working order. You should also make certain that the indicators and brake lights are functioning correctly and that there are no broken lenses. If replacements are needed they should be dealt with well before the test in case of any problems in the supply of spare parts. Although the test date could be a long time away, it is all too easy to be unprepared on the day if you do not make the necessary preparation early.

Lessons Sixteen to Twenty – Practice

Duration of lessons between one and two hours

We have now reached the stage where we can start thinking about the driving test and its problems.

You should now be thinking for yourself and acting on your own initiative. In fact, you are probably now up to the standard of the test in many ways. The only problem is that if anything goes wrong or you drive into any difficulty, you become flustered and unable to cope.

This is quite normal, and you only require more practice before you are really confident enough to take the test.

You must keep practising in as many difficult road and traffic conditions as possible, so make sure that your routes are as varied as possible.

The lessons can be for a longer duration from now on, as long as you do not get tired.

It is important that you still do not rush anything. Do everything in your own time. The main thing is that you do everything in the correct way. By now you should have read the Department of Transport booklet *HOW TO PASS THE DRIVING TEST*, which came with your licence. This is an excellent booklet which gives the details of the driving test and how you should drive to pass it. The booklet is set out under separate headings. These correspond with the headings on the driving test failure certificate, and the examiner's marking systems is based on them.

Many of these headings have already been covered in this course, but there are a few which we will now deal with, because they are relevant at this stage. They are set out under the same headings that you will find in the booklet and will assist you to understand them.

Meeting other vehicles safely   (See Fig. 37)

This situation arises when two vehicles 'meet' each other from opposite directions through a narrow gap.

Usually it is because parked cars have restricted the width of the road, which causes problems for other drivers.

The important thing is that you must always be prepared to give way to the other vehicle. You must therefore be looking well ahead and if there is any possibility of the other vehicle trying to go through the gap, you must slow down or stop.

The position in which you stop is very important.

It is of no use stopping where it would be inconvenient to either the other car or yourself.

Do not stop in a position so close to the parked vehicle or obstruction that you cannot continue when it is clear, without reversing or going too close to it.

The correct place to stop is well before the obstruction, far enough to the left for the other vehicle to move through unobstructed.

Before moving off again, make sure you check your mirror and signal if necessary.

Three points to remember:

1. Never keep going if there is any doubt at all as to whether there is enough room for two cars to get through the gap easily. Even if you have good judgement, the other person might not.
2. It is sometimes difficult to judge the speed of the oncoming car.
3. It is much safer to stop, even if you find, after stopping, that it may not have been necessary, than to try and get through a gap and cause an accident.

Learners always get into difficulties when meeting other vehicles, because they will never stop early enough.

You will learn best by the difficulties and by the mistakes that you make, so drive along plenty of narrow roads where there are parked vehicles.

One of the most common faults when meeting other vehicles is

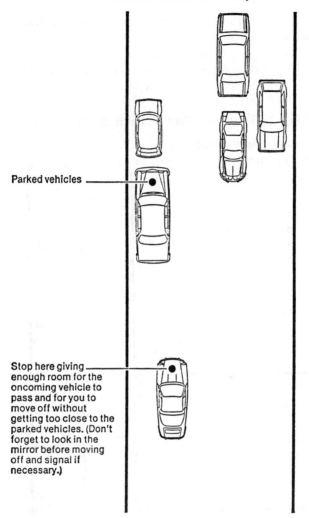

Parked vehicles ____

Stop here giving ____
enough room for the
oncoming vehicle to
pass and for you to
move off without
getting too close to the
parked vehicles. (Don't
forget to look in the
mirror before moving
off and signal if
necessary.)

Fig. 37   Meeting other vehicles safely.

that you will see the other car early, you will slow down, but will not actually stop. You find yourself creeping on at a very slow speed until you nearly hit the parked car.

One of the reasons for this is that you think that you have stopped, or that going at such a slow speed is the same as stopping. If necessary you must actually stop in the correct position, and not just think about stopping.

Another reason, perhaps, is that you still subconsciously do not want to stop because of all the 'performances' of moving off again. You have to try to get out of thinking in this way.

Cross the path of another vehicle safely   (See Fig. 38)

When you are turning right and have to cross the path of oncoming vehicles, you must leave yourself enough time to complete the

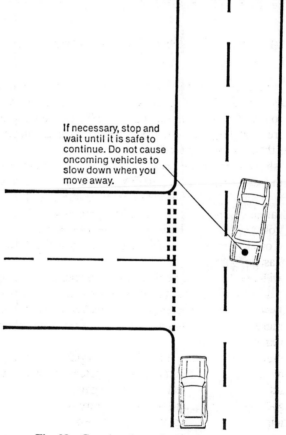

If necessary, stop and wait until it is safe to continue. Do not cause oncoming vehicles to slow down when you move away.

Fig. 38   Crossing the path of other vehicles.

manoeuvre safely. The problem is that it is difficult to judge the speed of an approaching vehicle, therefore you must allow for a large margin of error in your judgement.

Never try to 'nip' round the corner in front of somebody. Always stop if there is any doubt.

It is, of course, always a matter of opinion whether the pupil has left himself enough time to turn the corner safely. His judgement will not be very good so it is up to the instructor to guide him.

Remember that he needs much more time than you would, so always be certain that there is plenty of space between his turning and the approach of another vehicle.

If there is the slightest doubt in your mind, then tell him to wait.

Emerging with due regard for approaching traffic (See Fig. 39)

Exactly the same applies as when crossing the path of other vehicles. You must be sure that it is quite safe before you emerge from a side road into another road. This applies equally at roundabouts.

Be sure that you enter the road without causing danger to other vehicles that are already on the road.

You should not cause any vehicle to slow down or change direction (swerve out) either when you emerge from a side road or cross the path of anybody when entering another road.

All learners have difficulty in judging when to pull out at junctions. Your instructor will have to help you judge distances and speed of oncoming traffic at this stage, but try to judge for yourself as often as possible.

You will need much more time than an experienced driver would to pull out, and, of course, you must not cause any other vehicle to slow down for you even after you have moved into the road.

The most important thing is to be ready to move away as soon as there is an opportunity.

So often, you will have enough time to pull out but by the time you have accelerated, lifted the clutch, released the hand brake (if on), and looked right, left and right again, there is another car coming along the road, and the opportunity is lost.

Anticipate a likely gap in the traffic so that you are already accelerating and ready to go when the opportunity comes. The

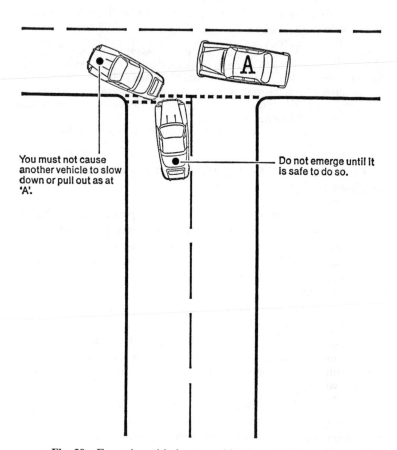

You must not cause another vehicle to slow down or pull out as at 'A'.

Do not emerge until It is safe to do so.

Fig. 39 Emerging with due regard for approaching traffic.

greatest difficulty often arises when turning right into a main road. You must be patient. Never pull out halfway across the road. Both ways must be clear before moving off. (The exception is a dual carriageway where you can move to the centre of the road and wait.)

As much practice as possible is required in pulling out of side roads into main roads for you to gain confidence in your own judgement.

Making progress to suit varying road and traffic conditions

In some ways this is connected with the above. It is important to be ready to move away when the opportunity arises. In other words, do not waste time at the end of roads. If you are waiting at the end of a road to move away, then be ready. Always have your acceleration correct and be ready to release your hand brake if you are on a hill. Try to anticipate when a likely opportunity is going to arise and take it.

Making progress means that once you have moved off, then you must increase your speed, and change up the gears at the right time. It is of no use if, after moving off, you stay for a long time in 1st or 2nd gear, thereby holding up other traffic. The earlier you can be travelling at about 28 mph in 4th gear the better (providing traffic conditions allow, of course). Always try to keep up with the flow of traffic, and if you are in a 40 or 50 mph speed limit, then you must increase your speed accordingly. But never go over the speed limit.

There is often a misconception that the learner must never go over 30 mph, even in higher speed limits. This is quite wrong. You should keep up your speed to near the limit where conditions allow, to keep up with the flow of traffic.

Making progress is one of the most difficult problems for learners. It is a very common cause of failing the test, and it is something that has no hard and fast rules about it. The pupil must be made aware of the fact that he is going too slowly, dawdling or taking too long to get out of a turning. He will tend to sit waiting to pull out, staring at a clear road, or when he has pulled out, drift slowly along in 1st or 2nd gear. Often at traffic lights he will be so slow that the lights change back to red again. You must never rush him, but gently persuade him to get a move on. If he thinks about making progress, then he will, but if he is just content to amble along the road, he will never improve.

Exercise proper care in the use of speed

This does not mean that you must not go over the speed limit, although this is important, because you would fail your test if you did. It also means that at all times you must be careful of your speed. Remember that you have a very heavy piece of machinery under your control, which can cause an awful lot of damage. 20 mph can be dangerously fast in some circumstances. Always endeavour to travel at a safe speed at all times and make sure that you approach slowly enough to be able to act correctly.

Pupils often do not realise the danger of speed and tend to think that provided they are travelling no faster than 30 mph they are safe. If at any time you consider that his speed is too high when approaching any hazard, then tell him immediately. Do not leave it or presume that he will slow down. It will be too late.

The emergency stop

For the reasons discussed in the introduction to the course we have left the emergency stop until this late stage of learning. A suitably quiet road should be found to practise it.

The procedure is as follows:

When you have reached the road in which you are going to practise the 'emergency stop', stop in a convenient position on the left. The instructor should then say something like:

We are now going to practise the emergency stop. When I bang my hand down on the dash-board I want you to stop the car as in an emergency, as though a child has run out in front of you.

As soon as my hand hits the dash-board you should apply the foot brake firmly, then depress the clutch. Make sure that you keep both hands on the steering wheel until the car has stopped. Do not go for the hand brake or gears until the car is stationary. Once you have stopped then apply the hand brake and put the gear into neutral.

I will make sure that it is safe to stop suddenly by checking behind as the examiner will in your test. You should not look in your mirror before stopping in this exercise.

Points to watch for

1. The important thing is how soon, not how hard, you put your foot on the brake after your instructor hits the dash-board; too many learners bang down the brake causing the car to skid violently. This must be avoided so it is better if, on the first couple of practices, you stop too slowly. This will give you the chance to become familiar with the feel of the foot brake when stopping suddenly. After a couple of attempts you will find it

easier to judge the amount of braking required. Remember that you should use 'progressive' braking when stopping (i.e. gradually increase the pressure on the brake, not just stamp on the brake).

2. Make sure that you keep both hands on the wheel until the car has stopped because although skidding should be avoided it is possible for the car to veer slightly one way or the other and therefore you must be in full control of the steering.

3. It is important that you depress the foot brake first, before the clutch. You may think that you will stall the engine but as long as you get your foot down on the clutch soon after the brake, the engine will keep running. If the clutch is applied first the car will not slow down as efficiently, in fact, if travelling down a hill it might even speed up slightly until the brake is used.

Make sure nothing is following by looking over your shoulder as well as in your mirror. The pupil should not look in his mirror, so it is up to you to make sure it is safe. Keep hold of the dash board when you bang your hand down to brace yourself in case he stops even more suddenly than you are expecting him to. (Remember the pupil has the steering wheel to hold on to, you have not.)

Practise the emergency stop a few times until you are happy with it. Try also to practise it in different weather conditions because you must not skid even on a wet road. If the car does skid you should release the foot brake for a moment and then depress it again. (This is also a good time to remind you that if the car skids to the right or left then you should turn the wheel into the skid. In other words if the back of the car skids to the left then turn the wheel to the left and vice versa.) See page 120.

Lessons Twenty-one to Twenty-five – Preparation

You should have the date of your driving test by now and therefore it is time to plan for the final preparations leading up to the test. The more practice that you can have from now on, the more chance you will have of passing. It is probably true that about 90% of the candidates who fail a driving test do so because of lack of practice.

You have now been taught everything that you need to know to be able to drive up to the standard for passing the test but you will still need more experience in the more difficult traffic conditions. Try to plan the lessons between now and the test so that they include some of the more difficult junctions and road hazards in your area.

In the next lessons your instructor should help you to prepare for the test by giving you a few check-tests, full details of which follow in the next lesson. These check-tests should be alternated with normal driving practice concentrating on any problems that you experience in the check-tests. Before the next lessons, however, you should read the following information on the driving test so that you are prepared for what is to follow. Your instructor should also read this because it is probably quite a long time since he took the test.

As the test approaches you can read the information about the test again as many times as you like to enable you to become familiar with the problems that you might encounter and how best to approach the 'ordeal' of the driving test.

On the day of the test you will need to have a lesson immediately before the test. You will find this on page 182.

The driving test

You will hear more tall stories and exaggerations concerning the driving test than almost anything else. This was mentioned in the introduction to this book and some of the reasons why the advice you hear is sometimes suspect were given then. As it is important for you to know what to expect when you are on test there follows some information that will prove very useful. You should also read the booklet entitled *How to Pass Your Driving Test* at this time even if you have read it before. There is also information about the test in *Driving* which you will find helpful.

Advice on taking the test

As can be seen from the check-test on page 171 of this course the Driving Test is always basically the same. There is a set pattern of manoeuvres and normal driving that is virtually the same for all tests; in fact even the examiner says almost exactly the same thing on every test. It could be said that the only things that change from one test to the next are the road, the traffic conditions and the *Highway Code* questions.

Examiner's attitude

It must be remembered that the examiner has to remain impartial and detached while he is conducting the test. Unfortunately the candidate sometimes thinks that he is being unfriendly towards him because he doesn't indulge in much conversation. The reason for the examiner's lack of conversation is that he is only supposed to give instructions for carrying out the test. He is not allowed to discuss the test or enter into conversation with the candidate. However, most examiners do try to put the candidate at ease wherever possible so don't think that the driving test is all that unfriendly.

Don't worry about the examiner writing things down

You will make mistakes on the test, everybody does, but do not let your mistakes put you off. The examiner considers each mistake on its merits and marks accordingly. He will not therefore fail you for the odd mistake here and there. He will decide whether the mistake was just a slip or something more serious such as lack of knowledge or competence. You must not dwell on the mistake because if you do you are liable to then make a far worse and more 'failable' mistake if you concentrate on the last incident and do not think about what is coming next.

Remember it is not necessarily the mistake that fails the candidate but what he does afterwards to rectify it. It can in fact sometimes help a person to pass a test if, even though he has made a mistake, he has shown that he remains calm, under control and then does the right thing to correct it.

Drive naturally

It is no use taking the test and driving in a different manner to that which you normally drive in an effort to try to impress the examiner. If you cannot pass the test by driving normally then you certainly will not pass it if you try to do things that you would not usually do. You should just drive in the way that you have been taught and in the way that is most natural to you.

This may seem strange to you at first glance but it is surprising how many people suddenly change the way that they drive, or change certain things in their driving, on the day of their test. You must just take everything as it comes and act in the way that you normally do.

Nerves

You will be nervous, especially at the beginning of the test. This usually wears off once you have driven for a few minutes. Don't worry about it because the examiner knows that you are nervous and takes this into account. Provided that you have had enough practice your nervousness will not affect your driving to a great extent.

Procedure of the test

The check-test will give you the procedure of the test from the time that the examiner enters your car. You should read it several times in the week or so before your test date so that you are familiar with it.

The following will help you to understand the full procedure of the test from the time that you reach the test centre.

1. You should arrive at the test centre about fifteen minutes before the scheduled time of the test to allow time to find a good parking position. (Always read the appointment card carefully to see if there are any instructions about parking such as a certain road or car park that you should use.)

2. Do not go into the test centre until five minutes before the test because sitting around in the waiting room for too long could make you even more nervous.

3. When you do go into the waiting room you should just sit and wait until the examiner comes in and calls out your name.

4. He will then ask you to sign a form, and invite you to lead him to your car.

5. Once outside the test centre he will ask if you have any physical disabilities that are not on your application form.

6. The eyesight test will come next.

   He will ask you to read the registration number of a random parked car. The car he chooses will probably be over the required 23 metres (25 yards). If you cannot read it he will get out a tape measure so that he can test you at exactly the required distance.

   Provided that you read the number correctly, he will:

7. Ask you to get into your car and make yourself comfortable. He will then walk round the car checking that the 'L' plates are attached and that the indicators and brake lights are in order. (You must make sure that the lens of the indicator and brake lights are not broken and that they are working correctly before you take your car for the test. The test will be cancelled if they are not.)

8. The examiner will then enter the car and sit beside you. This is the point at which the check-test on page 171 starts. It is at this point that the examiner will give you the instructions for proceeding on the driving part of the test and it is at this point that you should check that the doors are correctly shut, your seating position and mirror position are correct, seat-belt is on,

hand brake is on and gear is in neutral. It is no good going through your checking routine before he gets into the car because he would not see you.

The test would then proceed in much the same way as the check-test.

Tips for the test

1. Listen to the instructions given by the examiner. Do not presume that he is going to tell you to turn somewhere or do something; wait until he tells you.

2. If you stall the engine always apply the hand brake and put the gear into neutral before restarting the engine.

3. Never wave or command pedestrians to cross the road even at pedestrian crossings. He will fail you if you do.

4. Concentrate on your observation and positioning, especially at road junctions and crossroads (always get into the correct position and look right, left and right again before emerging).

5. Watch for unmarked crossroads.

   Whenever you are on a minor road it is quite possible to come across an unmarked crossroad where you must slow right down (2nd gear) and look properly.

6. Look for traffic signs that tell you that you must 'turn left', 'turn right' or that tell you that you are on a one-way street or an approaching dual-carriageway. Also look out for 'No Entry' signs. The examiner will not tell you to turn left or right if the traffic sign or road markings dictate that you should.

7. KEEP TO THE LEFT IN NORMAL DRIVING

   This is especially important when approaching junctions and roundabouts. Of course if the road markings dictate otherwise, or there is an obstruction in the left lane, you must position the car accordingly. On one-way roads that may fork with no road markings or indication as to which road is the main road always keep to the left.

8. Drive as naturally as possible using your common sense. For instance if you get to a mini-roundabout or junction and you stop to give the vehicle from the right his right of way and the driver of the vehicle then waits and indicates to you to go first, then provided that it is safe you should go. So many candidates

for a test just sit there while the other driver is waving them to go. One of you has to go eventually so although strictly speaking the other driver has the right of way, you should then go otherwise you will be holding up the rest of the traffic.

You can only stick to the rules of the road if other drivers let you. If they do not, you have to do the best that you can in the circumstances. This is always a very difficult situation for a candidate on a driving test but if you drive as naturally as possible then you have the best chance of passing your test.

Be positive. Let the examiner decide whether you did the correct thing in the circumstances.

9. Keep your wits about you! Remember that the test route is carefully planned out in advance therefore there is always a good reason why the examiner has asked you to turn into a particular road. He might want to see how you approach crossroads or mini-roundabouts that you are about to enter so keep your eyes open and think ahead otherwise you could miss something that may be crucial in passing or failing your test.

10. Give pedestrians plenty of room at all times. You must remember always to give way to pedestrians when you are turning at a junction if they are already crossing the road.

Lessons Twenty-one to Twenty-five – Practice

Duration of lessons between one and two hours

When you are within two or three weeks of your driving test and you are up to the standard of the test in every way it is important that you become familiar with the type of atmosphere that you will experience during the test.

When you take the test it will be the first time that you have had to drive the car with a stranger beside you who will not utter words of encouragement. Up until now you have become used to your instructor giving you advice and even helping you when things have gone wrong. On the test you will find it very different.

If you make a mistake you will have to put it right yourself. The only way to be ready for the test is to have had enough practice so that if a mistake is made (and remember nobody can drive for half an hour without making a mistake) then you are able to correct it without going to pieces.

It is not a good idea to keep going round the probable test route. This is not recommended by the Department of Transport because of the inconvenience caused to candidates actually taking their test, and to the people who live on the test route. Anyway, it is not much help because most test centres have so many routes that it would be pure luck if you happened to find the right one. In fact I have found that it can be off-putting to the candidate on test if he has expected to be taken on a certain route and is taken somewhere else instead.

What you can do with your instructor is try to find any hazards, such as a difficult junction, crossroads or a one-way system which is peculiar to that particular area and that could be used on the driving test. Talking to people who have taken their test at that centre often helps because they may be able to warn you of any particular hazards to look for.

Practice in the form of a check-test is a good idea because it will give you the idea of what it feels like to be actually on test with an examiner beside you. The aim of the check-test is to simulate the driving test as closely as possible with your instructor acting as the examiner.

It is a good idea to give two or three check-tests, interspersed with normal driving lessons.

The check-test

To do a check-test properly you must try to get into the right mood yourself. In other words, try to imagine that you are the examiner. Examiners are completely detached from the candidate, so you must endeavour when conducting a check-test, to become as detached as possible from your pupil.

Speak with a serious voice, give only the instructions that are necessary for directions and manoeuvres, and don't speak at any other time. If the pupil makes a mistake, then let him sort it out himself. Remember that in the test it is not always the mistake that causes failure, but what he did to correct it. In other words, it is his ability to correct mistakes that is so important. If you see that he is about to do something wrong do not interfere unless, of course, it could cause an accident.

You should make notes of any mistake during the check-test and then afterwards go over these with the pupil. Make sure you have a pen and paper with you.

Plan a route beforehand that would be suitable for a test. To make it as realistic as possible you must base it on the real test. The following points will help you to do this:

1. The test should last about thirty minutes.
2. Start the test at a similar type of road to the one at which the pupil will start the real test, i.e. main road, side road or even car-park if your particular test centre has one.
3. Try to include as many hazards as possible on your route: Plenty of small roads, left and right turns, road junctions, crossroads, one-way streets, at least one pedestrian crossing, roundabouts and traffic lights.
4. Find roads suitable to do an emergency stop, a reverse and a turn in the road.

All examiners in the actual driving test follow a certain procedure and order with their routes:

The first part of the test is straightforward driving to allow the candidate to settle down.

After about five minutes comes the emergency stop.

Then into the smaller roads with plenty of stopping, turning left and right and crossroads.

The reverse and the turn in the road then follow, usually in that order.

Then some more driving, including a hill start and moving off at an angle.

Then back to the test centre.

There now follows an explanation of a typical driving test. It includes the actual instructions that the examiner would give on a test and some problems that might arise. Use it as a basis for your check-test.

When you are at the starting point for your check-test you should switch the engine off. You are now the candidate.

You can assume your role as the examiner.

Have your pen and paper ready on your lap and put on your examiner's voice.

The check-test starts from the point when the examiner gets into the car.

Examiner: *Follow the road ahead unless the traffic signs direct you otherwise or unless I ask you to turn, which I will do in good time. Move off when you are ready, please.*

You should carry out the following checks before you switch the engine on:
1.   Check, and if necessary adjust the seat for correct positioning.
2.   Fasten your seat belt.
3.   Adjust mirror to correct position.
4.   Make sure the handbrake is on and the gear is in neutral.
5.   Check all doors are properly closed.

Try not to take too long over these checks. The seat and mirror should already be in the correct position so it should only be a matter of checking these. You should have made sure that your door is shut properly when you entered the car. Do not ask the examiner to lock his door but you can inquire if he is satisfied that his door is shut correctly, although this should not really be necessary because you can be certain that he will have checked this for himself.

Once you are satisfied that you have made the checks you can then switch on the engine and move off when it is safe to do so, after you have checked the mirror and looked over your shoulder. You should follow the road ahead as the examiner has told you. He will give you plenty of warning when he wants you to turn. If you approach a crossroads then follow the road straight ahead. Look for ONE-WAY directional signs and road markings because the examiner will expect you to obey these without his assistance.

Let the pupil settle down for a few minutes by taking him on some straightforward driving. At compulsory direction signs and road markings or when you want him to follow the road ahead at crossroads you should give no instruction. When you wish him to turn into another road you should give one of the following instructions, depending on the circumstances. Give your instruction early.

1. Would you take the next road on the left/right, please.
2. Will you take the second road off to the left/right, please. (As you are passing the first road you can say 'This is the first.')
3. At the end of the road turn left/right, please.

The first exercise will be the emergency stop. When you have reached the road in which you had planned to carry out the exercise give the following instruction:

Examiner: *Will you pull up on the left at a convenient place, please.*

You should stop as early as possible (after checking your mirror and signalling if necessary) in a good parking position. Do not stop on zig-zag school markings, next to somebody's driveway or at a bus stop.

Do not drive on too far after the examiner has asked

you to pull up. He will want you to stop as soon as it is convenient, not about half a mile up the road where it may be difficult for him to test the exercise. It can be very frustrating for an examiner if the candidate misses about five places where he could have pulled up conveniently. Try to keep your examiner happy!

Once you have pulled up in your convenient position put the handbrake on and gear lever into neutral. (Never switch the engine off unless the examiner asks you to, which will usually not be before the end of the test). The next instruction from the examiner will be:

Examiner: *Very shortly I shall ask you to stop as in an emergency. The signal will be like this.* (EXAMINER HITS DASHBOARD WITH BOOK AND SHOUTS 'STOP!') *When I do that I want you to stop immediately and under full control as though a child had run out in front of you. Do you understand? Drive on when you are ready, please.*

At the earliest opportunity the examiner will give the signal. He can only do this when it is safe, which could be some time, so you must drive normally until the signal is given. It is no good driving along very slowly waiting for it, because he will not give the signal unless you are driving at a normal speed (between 20 and 30 miles per hour), and he may fail you for 'not making normal progress'.

When the signal is given you should stop (without looking in the mirror) as quickly as possible by braking firmly and progressively. Depress the clutch just before you actually stop and keep both hands on the wheel to keep under full control. After you have stopped put the handbrake on and the gear lever into neutral.

You should not give the signal and shout STOP! until it is safe to do so and until the vehicle is travelling between 20 and 25 miles per hour. Look round over your shoulder to be absolutely sure that you will not endanger or inconvenience any other road user immediately before giving the STOP signal. When the pupil has stopped and applied the handbrake and put the gear lever into neutral you will say:

Examiner: *Thank you. I shall not ask you to carry out that exercise again. Drive on when you are ready please.*

The examiner will always say this so that there is no possibility of an accident being caused by the candidate mistakenly thinking that another emergency stop signal has been given.

When you move off after the emergency stop exercise remember to look in the mirror and round over both shoulders because you are probably in a stationary position in the centre of the road.

You will continue round the 'test' route until there is a suitable opportunity to carry out the 'MOVING OFF AT AN ANGLE' exercise.

Examiner: *Would you pull up just before you get to the next car on the left please. Leave enough room to move off.*

You should pull up about two metres (yards) before you reach the parked vehicle. (Whenever you are asked to pull up make sure you check the mirror early and signal if necessary.)

Examiner: *Drive on when you are ready, please.*

Check the mirror, look over your right shoulder, and if safe, give a right signal, before you move off round the parked vehicle. Keep control of the clutch until you have straightened the wheel after pulling out. Remember to watch for oncoming vehicles before you move off at an angle, especially if you are on a narrow road.

Continue round the route, leading towards the roads where the reverse and turn in the road are to be tested. If a suitable place to test the HILL-START is found, then it can be carried out before the other manoeuvres, or it can be left until afterwards if it is more convenient. The instruction if pulling up for the hill start is: 'Would you pull up on the left just along here, please.' Then 'Drive on when you are ready, please.'

When approaching the road where the reverse exercise is to be carried out give the following instruction:

Examiner: *Would you pull up just before you get to the next road on the left, please.*

Check your mirror and signal, if necessary, before you pull up just before the road on the left. Do not stop too close to the turning; try to be about 5 metres (yards) from the road in a good parking position.

Examiner: *This road on the left is the one I'd like you to reverse into. Drive past it and stop. Then back in and continue to drive in reverse gear for some distance, keeping reasonably close to the kerb.*

You should move forward (after looking in your mirror and over your right shoulder) to a position just a few metres (yards) past the corner and just under one metre (between 2 and 3 feet) from the kerb.

Then proceed with the reverse exercise, taking care to observe correctly; that is, looking all round before moving off, looking out of the front just before beginning to actually turn the corner, and generally looking out for pedestrians who could be endangered by your manoeuvre.

If any vehicle or pedestrian is endangered, you must stop, wait until the danger has gone, then continue with the exercise. Do not attempt to go round parked vehicles after you have turned the corner. Just stop before you reach any obstruction, keeping reasonably close to the kerb. Keep control of the clutch throughout the manoeuvre.

Because of the stress of taking a test, you may find that you do not straighten the car up as well as usual after turning the corner, thereby finding yourself close to the kerb. If you touch the kerb or feel that you are about to do so you should stop, select 1st gear and move forward a distance, and then continue with your reverse. This will enable you to move out from the kerb and is quite permissible on test. Remember, a mistake on test will not necessrily fail you provided that you correct it.

Continue reversing, keeping control of the clutch and steering, until the examiner asks you to pull up. Then the examiner will say:

Examiner: *Drive on when you are ready and at the end of the road turn right/left.*

Before you move off after the reversing exercise make sure that you look in the mirror and over your right shoulder. Also when you arrive at the end of the road remember to look RIGHT, LEFT and RIGHT again before you emerge into the other road. For some reason candidates often forget this immediately after the reverse – probably because they are still thinking about the exercise. If you removed your seat belt for the reverse manoeuvre do not forget to put it back on. If you do forget, then pull up on the left safely, telling the examiner what you are doing, so that you can put it on.

Continue round the test route until you reach the road where the turn in the road exercise is to be tested.

Examiner: *Would you pull up on the left just past the next lamp-post, please.*

Look in the mirror and signal if necessary.

Examiner: *I'd like you to turn your car round to face the opposite direction by using your forward and reverse gears. Try not to touch the kerb while you are turning.*

Remember clutch control and observation are vital. (Look in the mirror and over your right shoulder before moving off; look right and left before moving off from each side of the road and look out of the back while reversing).

When you have completed the exercise the examiner will usually ask you to continue without pulling up. If you have removed your seat belt for the manoeuvre you should pull up on the left to put it on.

Continue on the route leading back towards the 'test centre' (starting place). If it has not been possible to carry out any exercise such as hill start, etc., you may now find an opportunity to do so. When you reach the test centre:

Examiner: *Would you pull up on the left at a convenient place, please.*

Look in your mirror and signal if necessary. Find a good safe parking position in which to pull up.

Examiner: *You can switch your engine off.*
Now I'd like to put a few questions on the Highway Code *and other motoring matters.*

The practical part of the test has now ended and the examiner will then ask you about five *Highway Code* questions and ask you to identify several road signs which he will show you from a book.

He would then tell you if you had passed or failed and fill out the appropriate form.

You can now go over the things that you did wrong with your instructor, who will explain any problems that arose on the check-test.

It is not a good idea to do much more driving after the check-test; just drive home. It is advisable to practise any problems that have come to light when you next have a lesson.

When you have had a couple of ordinary lessons try another check-test.

Go over the check-test with the pupil and make a note of any items that need practice in the future. These can then be practised in the next lesson.

The Lesson Before the Test and the Driving Test – Preparation

You should now be fully prepared for the driving test and be reasonably confident of your own driving ability. You are, of course, still inexperienced but with the practice that you have had you will be able to cope with any problem that might arise on your test. You will probably make mistakes but if you try to relax and keep calm you will be able to correct anything that you do wrong. You will also be nervous but this should not affect your driving to a very great extent. Remember that the examiner only wants to see that you are up to a reasonable standard of driving to enable you to drive on your own safely. He knows that you are inexperienced so he is not expecting you to be the best driver in the world but he does expect you to obey the rules of the road, act responsibly when driving and to be at the standard set down by the Department of Transport. You should, by now, have reached this standard, therefore if you drive as naturally as you can and keep your wits about you, you should not fail.

You should read the notes on the driving test (page 165) again just before the test and in the week before read up on any points in the book which you think might be helpful. You should also read again the booklet *Your Driving Test and How to Pass It.*

At the end of the driving test the examiner will ask you approximately six questions on *The Highway Code.* These questions will not usually be the obvious questions such as 'where must you not park or overtake' because the examiner can see, by the way you drive, if you have a basic knowledge of *The Highway Code.* He is more likely to ask the kind of questions that will test your understanding of and reasoning behind the rules laid down in *The Highway Code*, and your general knowledge of driving.

He will also possibly ask you questions on the types of roads and conditions that you have not been tested on, but that you could experience if you pass the test. These include motorway driving, driving at night and driving in fog or in icy conditions. All of these are explained in this book (motorways you will find in the appendix at the back) so you should read them all before the test.

The examiner will often ask questions concerning road signs by showing you a sign in his book and asking you to tell him the meaning of it.

There follow several questions on *The Highway Code*. These are the type of questions that the examiner could ask but of course you will be lucky if he actually asks you any one of these on the day. It will, however, give you an idea as to what the examiner is looking for in the oral part of the test. (Answers on page 185.)

Highway Code Questions

1. If you are approaching traffic lights and the amber light comes on, what should you do?
2. What is the sequence of traffic lights starting and ending at green?
3. What does the flashing amber light at a 'pelican' crossing mean?
4. What is the zig-zag white line near a zebra crossing for and what is the law regarding this line?
5. How would you know that you were approaching a zebra crossing?
6. What is the acceleration lane on a motorway?
7. If you were driving on a motorway at the maximum speed allowed and there was no other traffic near you, which lane should you be in?
8. If you missed the road that you intended to take off the motorway what would you do?
9. If there is a double white line along the centre of the road and the continuous line is on your side of the road what must you do?
10. What are box junctions?

11. Where would you find the chevron sign?
12. What is the first thing that you should do before turning right?
13. If it is foggy during daylight what precautions should you take?
14. Where should you not park your vehicle at night although you can park there at most times during the day?
15. When and for what reasons should a driver flash his lights?
16. What is the overall stopping distance if you were travelling at 50 mph?
17. What are the primary causes of skidding?
18. If you were following a large vehicle along a road and it was not safe to overtake it at that moment, what should you do?

The Lesson Before the Test – Practice

This is a very important lesson, because not only must it include some practice of normal driving and manoeuvres, but it must also help to get you into the right frame of mind for the test. In other words, it must settle your nerves and build up your confidence.

You should set out from home about one hour before the scheduled time of the test. Any longer would make him tired by the time the test was due; less time might not be enough.

Route

The route must include roads suitable for practising the turn in the road, reverse and emergency stop. It should also include any difficult hazards that you know in the vicinity of the test area. It is well worth working out a route beforehand, but remember to keep it relatively short.

Procedure

1. Before setting out, make sure that you have your driving licence and appointment card with you. (Although the licence does not have to be produced before the test the examiner will want to see it if you pass.)
2. Take the lesson nice and easy; try not to rush. Do not worry if you make mistakes during this pre-test lesson. (It is better to make mistakes before the test than actually on the test.)
3. Keep to the quiet roads for a few minutes at the beginning of the lesson to help settle your nerves.

4. Practise a turn in the road, a reverse, an emergency stop, a hill start and moving off at an angle. Do not overdo any of these manoeuvres. If possible, just stick to one of each unless you do something so badly on a manoeuvre that you feel you must have another try to restore your confidence.

   If you do a reasonable manoeuvre, then drive on to something else.

5. Do not try to learn anything new or different on this lesson. The lesson must be used solely for practice.

6. Make sure that you arrive at the parking place outside the test centre about fifteen minutes before the test is due.

7. Do not go into the test centre waiting room until five minutes before the test. (You will become more nervous if you have to sit around for too long in the atmosphere of a waiting room.)

8. You should both sit in the car for ten minutes or so before you go into the test centre, and use the time by asking him some *Highway Code* questions, and giving him a few last-minute tips about looking properly at crossroads and taking his time.

9. Go with the pupil into the test centre and wait with him until the examiner calls him. He will need you for comfort and moral support.

Appendix I: After the test

To the pupil

After the test

If you passed your test you should try to practise as soon as possible. There is much to learn but you can now gain experience and at the same time build up your confidence. Take things steady at first, then gradually drive in more difficult conditions on busy roads including dual-carriageways and motorways if possible.

If you did not pass the test, don't worry about it too much. It is not a bad thing to be reasonably certain that you are safe to drive on your own and you now have the chance to have more valuable practice with your instructor before the next test. It is most likely that you failed because of lack of practice (of the 22,000 people who fail a driving test every year about 90% do so because of lack of practice). You should read the form that the examiner gave you before your next lesson. This form is very helpful as it tells you exactly what the examiner considered to be the faults in your driving. Read it very carefully with your instructor making sure that you see exactly what faults the examiner has underlined. You must then look up the corresponding headings in this book and in the Ministry booklet *How to Pass Your Driving Test* to understand fully the correct meaning of the examiner's markings.

Fill in and send the application form for the next test as soon as possible and after a week's rest from driving you should start the lessons again. I have suggested a week's break because you will probably want to forget about driving for a short time but if you feel like driving straight away and you have the opportunity then go ahead and practise.

Very often the pupil does not feel like driving for a week or so after failing a test. You should not force him to drive until he wants to unless, of course, the break lasts for a month in which case a lot of encouragement may be needed.

You will need to work up to the next test, therefore, once you have gone over the points on which you failed the last test you should concentrate upon general practice including all the procedures and manoeuvres for the test. Plenty of practice in the more difficult traffic conditions interspersed with some check-tests in the four weeks prior to the test will give you every chance of passing next time. You should restart the course at Lesson 6 as preparation for the test but you can refresh your memory on any points in the first half of the book that may have been a contributory factor in failing the last test.

Highway Code (Answers)

1. You must stop at the white stop line at the traffic lights unless you are so close to the stop line that to stop would cause an accident.
2. Green, amber, red, red and amber together, green.
3. You must give way to any pedestrians on the crossing; otherwise you may proceed.
4. It is to warn of the approach of a 'zebra' crossing. You must not stop in the area marked by the zig-zag lines except to give precedence to a pedestrian on the crossing, or to wait to turn right or left, or in circumstances beyond your control, or when it is necessary to avoid an accident. In the area marked with zig-zag lines on the approach to a zebra crossing, you must not overtake the moving vehicle nearest the crossing, or the leading vehicle which has stopped to give way to a pedestrian on the crossing.
5. You would see the flashing yellow beacons; the zig-zag white lines on the approach side of the crossing and the black and white stripes of the crossing itself.
6. It is an extra lane at the side of the motorway that continues on

from the slip road as you enter the motorway. This lane enables you to adjust your speed so that when you join the motorway you are already travelling at the same speed as the other traffic. If there is not a suitable gap in the traffic you must wait in the acceleration lane until it is safe to enter the motorway.

7. The lefthand lane.

8. Continue driving until you reach the next exit on the left of the motorway. You can then go over the bridge and rejoin the motorway in the opposite direction if necessary.

9. You must not cross or straddle the continuous white line unless you are turning in or out of a side road; or when you have to avoid a stationary obstruction. You must not stop, except to avoid an accident, on any section of road marked with double white lines.

10. Box junctions have criss-cross yellow lines painted on the road. You must not enter the box if your exit road or lane from it is not clear. But you may enter the box when you want to turn right and are prevented from doing so only by oncoming traffic or by vehicles making a right turn.

11. Where there is a sharp deviation of the road (e.g. bends, roundabouts). At roadworks showing sharp temporary deviation of the road.

12. Look in the mirror.

13. Drive more slowly; keep further back from the vehicle in front; drive with headlights on or/and fog lights; use windscreen wipers; allow more time for your journey.

14. On the wrong side of the road. (In fog you should not park on the wrong side of the road during daylight.)

15. If you wish to let another road user know you are there. When travelling at high speeds it is a good idea to use the flashing lights signal instead of sounding the horn to warn others of your presence because the sound of the horn would be lost.

16. About 54 metres (175 feet) in good conditions.

17. Harsh braking, sudden acceleration or turning the steering wheel too quickly for the prevailing conditions.

18. Keep far enough behind the vehicle to be able to see ahead of it so that you are in a position to decide when it is safe to overtake. By being further back behind the vehicle you can

also see any dangers ahead and therefore be ready to act in good time.

Note on Metrication

Throughout this book I have given distances in both metres and yards. The conversions are approximate and are intended for guidance only. Road, traffic and weather conditions all play a part in determining stopping and braking distances. In every situation you must exercise your own judgement for safe driving.

Appendix II: Motorway driving

Motorway driving

Motorways are different in many ways from any other road because they are designed to carry a large amount of traffic at higher than average speed as safely as possible for long distances. There are, therefore, certain rules and restrictions that apply to a motorway which differ from the rules for other roads. One of these restrictions applies to learner drivers. It states that learner drivers are not allowed on the motorway except for HGV learners (heavy goods vehicles). The reason is that an inexperienced learner could cause danger to other motorists because of his lack of practice at the higher speeds required on a motorway.

This, of course, is a sensible restriction, but how then are you ever going to get practice on a motorway?

You will just have to wait until you have passed the driving test and then, when the opportunity arises, pluck up the courage and have a go. If you can, choose a weekend as there is less heavy goods traffic. Never make your first drive on a motorway in bad weather conditions (e.g. fog or heavy rain). Before you start out make sure that you know the rules and restrictions and that you are prepared for some of the problems that can arise when driving on a motorway.

Restrictions
The following are not allowed on a motorway:

Pedestrians
Learner drivers except HGV learners

Cyclists and riders of small motorcycles under 50 cc capacity
Slow-moving vehicles carrying outsized loads (unless permission
is obtained)
Agricultural vehicles
Invalid carriages not exceeding 5 cwt unladen weight
Animals (including horse and cart, etc.)

When on a motorway you *must not*:

Exceed 70 mph.
Reverse on the carriageways.
Stop on the carriageways.
Stop on the verges except in an emergency.
Stop on or cross the central reservation.
Walk on the carriageways or on the central reservation except in
an emergency.

How to deal with the problems that may arise on a motorway

Overtaking

You must be aware that the traffic is moving faster than you have
been used to when you first drive on a motorway otherwise you
might make fatal errors of judgement when changing lane and
overtaking. The same procedure as on any road is necessary before
you overtake another vehicle but you must look in your mirror
earlier, signal earlier and allow much more time for the manoeuvre.

When you look in your mirror on a motorway you have to
consider the distance and speed of following vehicles, especially the
vehicles on the outer lanes, because your judgement for overtaking
will depend on this. Do not presume that the vehicle you see in your
mirror is travelling slightly faster than you. It could be travelling
three times as fast as you because unfortunately not everybody
keeps to the speed limits. You can imagine what would happen if
having checked in your mirror you decided that the driver behind
was travelling at 50 mph at a distance of 150 metres (160 yards) and
in fact was travelling at 120 mph at a distance of 100 metres (110
yards). If you pulled out into his lane he would have no chance to do
very much about it at that speed.

It is vital that you look more than once in the mirror to decide if it
is safe to overtake because by doing this you can judge how much

nearer the vehicle behind is since you last looked. This will give you a good idea of the speed at which it is travelling. IF IN DOUBT, DON'T PULL OUT!

Anticipation

It is even more important to look a long way ahead so that you can anticipate and act on any possible hazard. Danger occurs so quickly on a motorway that you must be fully prepared as early as possible. As soon as you see any possible danger ahead you must immediately take your foot off the accelerator; a split second can make all the difference when avoiding an accident.

Possible danger signs are:

Bunching of vehicles ahead.
A vehicle ahead weaving in and out at speed thereby causing other vehicles to take evasive action.
Any brake lights coming on ahead.
Several large vehicles overtaking each other ahead.

There are many more danger signs which you will learn to take notice of with more experience on the motorway.

Entering the motorway

You will enter the acceleration lane when you come off the slip road when entering a motorway. The acceleration lane is there to let you increase your speed so that it matches the speed of the traffic already on the motorway. With practice you will be able to judge the speed that you will need to move into the motorway safely but you must also be ready to slow right down if there is no room for you to enter a very busy motorway. Do not just keep going regardless of the traffic situation.

Once on the motorway you must then adjust to the different speeds and driving conditions before you attempt to go too fast or overtake.

Leaving the motorway

Look out for the direction signs so that you can get into the left lane early before leaving the motorway. Then look out for the 'count down' markers because they are there to tell you exactly how far away the exit road is.

Once off the motorway you must adjust your speed and driving to suit normal roads. A quick glance at your speedometer is essential because it is very difficult to judge lower speeds if you have been travelling a long way at higher speeds.

Signalling

You must give any signals that may be necessary very early. Once having given the signal you must look in the mirror again to make sure that it is still safe before you move out or in.

Use flashing headlights instead of the horn to warn other motorists you are there because at high speeds the sound of the horn could possibly not reach others.

Further preparation before driving on a motorway

Before ever driving on a motorway you must read the motorway section in *The Highway Code*. This will give you all the rules that you must obey.

Appendix III: Parking

Parking in a limited space between two cars
(See Fig. 40)

This is a manoeuvre that causes many problems. It is not required to be performed during the driving test because it is impractical to find a suitable place to test it on the open road in the context of the test.

It is not as difficult to park a car in a limited space as is thought. After all, if a driver can control the car well enough to do the turning in the road and reverse round the corner he should be capable of parking. The problem is really just lack of practice. This is because the first attempts at this sort of parking are usually performed in the most difficult conditions (in the middle of a busy street where there is very limited time as well as space).

Early practice
Either just before or after passing the driving test you should, with your instructor, practise this manoeuvre. Find a nice quiet road and two vehicles parked at the side of the road about two car lengths apart. (If you don't want to risk doing your first attempt with cars, then place two boxes the correct distance apart.) You can gradually reduce the distance between the two cars to about one and a half lengths. There is no reason to attempt this manoeuvre in less space; in fact one of the reasons that drivers have so much trouble parking is that they attempt it in too small a space.

Procedure
It is necessary to reverse into the space so you must stop about half a

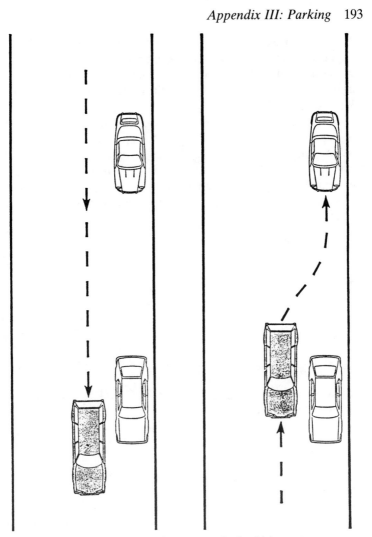

Fig. 40 Parking between parked vehicles.

car length past the gap parallel with the first car and about one metre (3 feet) out from it. Observation is very important so you must look all round before reversing. Be aware that the front of your car will move out a long way into the road as you move into the gap causing danger to oncoming vehicles. When you are satisfied that it is safe, proceed.

Reverse slowly, turning the wheel slightly to the left. Aim for the nearside front corner of the rear parked car.

When the front of your car has cleared the rear of the forward parked car turn the wheel quickly to the right. You may have to use full right lock at this point.

Continue reversing slowly and straighten wheel as necessary. You can then move forward to straighten up if necessary.

When you have practised this manoeuvre several times, in different, but similar spaces, you can then try it in a busier place. Remember, though, that it can be an inconvenience to others where there are heavy traffic conditions in busy shopping centres.

Appendix IV: Automatic transmission

Automatic transmission

It is a common misconception that it is much easier to learn how to drive and to pass the driving test in a vehicle fitted with automatic transmission. It is true that it is easier to actually move off from a stationary position because there is no clutch to worry about, but all the other problems that the learner encounters remain much the same.

The trouble is that the word 'automatic' conveys to the beginner an idea that there is nothing for him to do except switch the engine on, put his foot on the accelerator, steer and the car will do the rest by itself. This is far from the truth and the following notes will help to explain why this is.

Gears

The understanding of the gears in an 'automatic' is as important as in a 'manual' car because although there is the possibility to allow the vehicle to select its own gear changes there are times when the selection of gears must be done by the driver. There are different types of automatic transmission available, so it is therefore impossible to explain the exact method used on all cars. It is possible, however, to generalise on the most common types of automatic transmissions but it is essential to study the handbook for the particular car before attempting to drive the car.

Selector lever

Most 'automatics' have a selector lever which enables you to select the gear required. The range of gears available to be selected depends on the type of car but most selectors have the following positions:

N.   (Neutral)
This corresponds with the neutral position in a 'manual' car. When the selector lever is in this position the engine can be started.

R.   (Reverse)
This enables the vehicle to be driven backwards with only one gear as in a 'manual' car.

D.   (Drive)
This position enables the vehicle to be driven forward. In most cars it is not possible to start the engine when the selector is in the 'drive' or 'reverse' position.

Once the engine is started in 'neutral' the 'drive' position can then be selected and when the brakes are released the vehicle can be driven forward by applying pressure on the accelerator pedal. As the pressure on the accelerator pedal is increased the vehicle will automatically change gear in relation to the changes in road speed. The actual road speed at which the gears will change depends upon the amount of pressure applied to the accelerator pedal. With heavy pressure on the accelerator pedal the gear change will be at a higher road speed than it would be if a light pressure is applied. The reason for this is that the gear change is not only determined by road speed but also by the load on the engine to allow the gear change to be delayed when climbing a steep hill. With most 'automatics', therefore, it is better to use gentle pressure on the accelerator pedal for smooth gear changes. Although most automatic transmission vehicles have three gears there are some with only two and others with four gears. As the road speed decreases below a certain level, or the load on the engine increases, the mechanism will automatically change the transmission into a lower gear.

L.   (Lock up or Hold)
This enables the driver to override the automatic transmission so that a lower gear can be selected and held. This is useful when travelling in very slow moving traffic because unnecessary gear changes that could occur in the 'drive' position might make it more difficult to control the car. This 'lock up' position can also be used

when descending a steep hill to keep the car in a low gear for control over speed. Once the 'lock up' position is selected the higher gear will not be engaged until 'drive' position is selected again.

P. (Park)

This locks the transmission when the vehicle is parked. It should be used after the hand brake is applied and the engine is switched off.

Other selector positions

In some vehicles with automatic transmission there are other possible selections. One possible variation is the 'D1' and 'D2' replacement for the normal 'D' position. When 'D2' is selected it cuts out the lowest gear and therefore the vehicle is moved off from a stationary position in 2nd gear. This is useful if the road surface is slippery and greater traction is required for a slow, smooth start.

Some automatic transmissions have all four gears, as in a manual vehicle, which can be selected as required.

Kick down

When the accelerator pedal is pressed suddenly and fully down the automatic mechanism is overridden and the next lower gear is engaged. This is very useful when extra acceleration is required for overtaking. The automatic mechanism is re-engaged when the pressure is eased off the accelerator pedal.

Foot pedals   (accelerator and brake)

These are the only two foot pedals in a vehicle with automatic transmission. They should normally both be controlled with the right foot when driving along. When manoeuvring at a very slow speed, however, it is convenient, and quite safe, to control the car by using a slight amount of acceleration with the right foot while using the brake with the left foot.

Accelerator

Pressure on the accelerator pedal increases the engine speed and therefore the speed of the car when 'drive' or 'reverse' are selected.

As stated earlier, when we were discussing the gears, the pressure applied to the accelerator pedal when the gear selector is in the drive position controls to a certain extent, the way in which the gears are automatically changed. Practice on the accelerator pedal is essential to enable the car to be controlled safely in all situations.

One major difference between an automatic and a manual car is that whereas the engine will slow down the road speed of the car when the foot is lifted off the accelerator in a manual car this does not happen in most 'automatic' vehicles.

Foot brake

The correct use of the foot brake on an automatic transmission vehicle is even more vital than on a 'manual' car because the engine will not help to slow the car down when the pressure on the accelerator is lifted, therefore all the slowing down must be done with the foot brake. It is equally important to use 'progressive' (see page 40) braking and it is essential to start braking very early. When any danger is seen the right foot must be lifted off the accelerator and on to the brake immediately to enable the necessary adjustment of speed to be made as early as possible.

Hand brake

This is very important because once either position 'D' 'L' or 'R' is engaged the vehicle will move off as soon as the accelerator is pressed unless the brakes are on. In fact the vehicle could move off under power even without the accelerator being depressed if the choke is on or the tick-over is too fast. The hand brake should therefore be applied whenever the vehicle is stationary.

'Creep'

This term is used to describe the effect that the tick-over of the engine will have on the car. If there is excessive 'creep' the car will move off without any pressure being applied to the accelerator pedal even when the choke is not being used. When you first drive an 'automatic' vehicle you should test the amount of 'creep' and if it is excessive the tick-over should be checked.

You should never rely on the 'creep' to hold the car stationary on an incline. Always use the hand brake.

Other problems to watch for when driving an automatic

Approaching junctions

There is a tendency for many 'automatics' to change up a gear as you approach a corner because of the reduction of pressure on the accelerator pedal. Provided that the routine for approaching bends and junctions (pages 28–40) is adhered to there should be no problem. The correct use of 'progressive' braking is vitally important when approaching a sharp corner in an 'automatic' especially when descending a hill and the use of L (lockup) will help to control the car when gentle acceleration is applied as the corner is turned. The selection of any gear must, of course, be completed before the corner is reached.

General driving

Everything discussed in this book concerning control, observation and positioning applies equally to the driver of a car with an automatic transmission as to the driver of a car with manual transmission.

Index